# ZHAN ZHUAN
## THE ART OF NOURISHING LIFE

# DISCOVERY PUBLISHER

Original Edition
Original Title: "站桩养生法"
2014, Discovery Publisher

For the English edition:
©2015, Discovery Publisher
All rights reserved.

No part of this book may be reproduced in any form or by any electronic or mechanical means including information storage and retrieval systems, without permission in writing from the publisher.

**Author**: Dr. Yu Yongnian 于永年
**Translators**: Zhang Yingzhu 张影竹, Brittany Leotaud
**Editor**: Gitanjali Kurugodu
**Prologue & Interview**: Karim Nimri
**Editor in Chief**: Adriano Lucchese

### DISCOVERY PUBLISHER

616 Corporate Way, Suite 2-4933
Valley Cottage, New York, 10989
www.discoverypublisher.com
books@discoverypublisher.com
facebook.com/DiscoveryPublisher
twitter.com/DiscoveryPB

New York • Tokyo • Paris • Hong Kong

# TABLE OF CONTENTS

## PROLOGUE — 1

### Prologue — 3

- The end of an era of superstitions — 3
- The transformation of martial arts — 3
  - Reinterpretation of art in Republican China: the Guo Shu Era — 4
  - Central National Academy of Arts of Nanjing — 5
  - Wang Xiangzhai — 5
  - The People's Republic of China: The Wu Shu of sports and health — 5
  - The Research Association of Chinese Kung Fu in Peking — 6
  - Yu Yongnian: The art of Intention — 6

## INTERVIEW WITH DR. YU YONGNIAN — 11

### Interview with Dr. Yu Yongnian — 13

- The Power of Peace — 13

## ZHAN ZHUAN: THE ART OF NOURISHING LIFE — 27

### Chapter I: Introduction — 29

- 1. Medical effects of Standing Like a Tree — 29
- 2. Reactions after Standing Like a Tree — 32

| | |
|---|---|
| a. Sensations of pins and needles and aches | 32 |
| b. Feeling of painful swelling | 33 |
| c. Feeling of heat | 33 |
| d. Feeling of vibrations | 33 |
| e. Feeling of difference | 34 |
| f. Feeling of well-being and joy | 35 |
| 3. Precautions to take during the training | 36 |

## Chapter II: Upright Position — 41

| | |
|---|---|
| 1. Different positions in Standing Like a Tree | 41 |
| 2. Main positions in Standing like a Tree; standing | 43 |

## Chapter III: How does one master the intensity of the Zhan Zhuang movement? — 49

| | |
|---|---|
| 1. The choice between the practice of the hand or the foot | 49 |
| 2. Classification of the different intensities of movement | 52 |
| a. Intensity Without Effect | 53 |
| b. Maintained Intensity | 53 |
| c. Reinforced Intensity | 54 |
| d. Excessive Intensity | 54 |
| e. Insufficient Intensity | 54 |
| 3. Movement Intensity Factors | 55 |
| a. The Subjective Factor | 55 |
| b. The Objective Factor | 55 |
| c. The Duration Factor | 56 |
| d. The Recovery Period Factor | 56 |
| 4. Calculation of the Intensity of Movement | 57 |
| a. Calculation of height in cm | 57 |

b. Calculation in mm of the vertical projection from the body's centre of gravity …… 57
  c. Calculation of the spiritual activities in μm …… 58

5. The principle of adjustment and distribution on Yi (purpose) and Xing (posture) …… 58

  a. Eliminating Yi and suppressing Xing …… 59
  b. Eliminating Yi and exaggerating Xing …… 59
  c. Reducing Yi and Xing at the same time …… 59
  d. Reducing Yi and increasing Xing …… 59
  e. Exaggerating Yi and suppressing Xing …… 59
  f. Increasing Yi and Xing at the same time …… 60

6. Coordination or Xing (posture), YI (Intention), Li (strength), Qi (energy) and Shen (vigour) …… 60

  a. Having Xing without I is an "Empty Xing" …… 60
  b. Having I without Xing does not increase strength …… 60
  c. Having Yi without Li is an "Empty Yi" …… 60
  d. Having strength without I is inefficient …… 61
  e. Having strength without Qi is a banal strength …… 61
  f. Having Qi without strength is not practical …… 61
  g. Having I without Shen is not of the highest level …… 61
  h. Having Shen – Yi – Li – Qi, always be prepared …… 62

7. Relationship between the degree of flexion and the intensity of movement …… 62

  a. Relationship between the pivot point and the intensity of movement …… 62
  b. Relationship between the surface of the foot and the intensity of movement …… 63
  d. Relationship between the position of the knee joint and the intensity of movement …… 67
  e. Relationship between the position of the hip joint and the intensity of movement …… 68

f. Relationship between the position of the ankle joint and the intensity of movement — 69
g. Relationship between the position of the shoulder joint and the intensity of movement — 69
h. Relationship between the position of the elbow joint and the intensity of movement — 70
i. Relationship between the position of the wrist and the intensity of movement — 70

## Chapter IV: The Work of Intention in Zhan Zhuang — 73

1. The Action of Relaxation — 73

    a. Relaxation of the mind — 74
    b. Relaxation of expression — 74
    c. Relaxation by breathing — 74
    d. Relaxation by small movement — 75
    e. Relaxation by actively changing position — 75
    f. Relaxation by passively changing position — 75

2. The Action of Imagination — 76

    a. Looking into the distance — 76
    b. Listening from a distance — 76
    c. Holding an object — 76
    d. Walking on cotton — 77
    e. Holding a balloon in the arms — 77
    f. Moving forward in water — 77

3. Flexible muscle movement — 78

    a. Introduction — 78
    b. Flexible leg movement — 78

4. Action of connecting — 81

    a. Tip of the foot-heel-knee — 82
    b. Tip of the foot-knee-hip — 82

    c. Knee-stomach-hip; tip of foot-heel-knee-stomach-hip-buttocks   82
    d. Elbow-shoulder-hand   82
    e. Thumb-little finger-wrist   83

  5. The action of pulling the tendon   83

    a. Both feet / back   83
    b. Both feet / neck   84
    c. Both hands / neck   84
    d. Both feet / back; both hands / back   84

## Chapter V: The Theory of Zhan Zhuang   87

  1. The relation Between Medicine and Physical Activities   87

  2. Diagram explaining how Zhan Zhuang works and its evolution of work   88

  3. Discussion on the definition of stability and movement in stability   90

    a. Definition of movement and stability   91
    b. Classification of movement   92

  4. Application of flexible movement to "contraction and relaxation" exercises of the bottom of the foot   94

    a. Passive movement   94
    b. Active movement   95
    c. Role of the sole of the foot   96
    d. Action of the sole of the foot in static position   97
    e. The movement of running   99
    f. The movement of jumping   100
    g. The movement of "Stretching / Tightening"   101
    h. The movement of "Sliding / Stopping"   102
    i. The movement of "Crushing / Rubbing"   103

j. The movement of "Pulling / Lifting" — 103

## Chapter VI : A Study on Qi (Energy) — 107

1. What is Qi? — 107

   a. Qi is a magnetic wave — 108
   b. Qi is a low frequency infra-red wave — 108
   c. Qi's field — 109

2. Commentaries from abroad — 111

   a. Report from the Committee of Science of the United States — 111
   b. Discover report — 112

3. Test of External Qi — 113

   a. Effects of external Qi — 113

## Chapter VII : A Study on the "Object" — 114

1. What is the "Object"? — 114

2. The object described by Laozi — 116

3. Relations between Qi (Energy), Strength, Object and Tao — 118

4. To forget while in a seated position and to create in Tao — 119

5. The most important use of the "Object" — 121

6. The "Object" of Yi Quan — 122

## Chapter VIII : The Quest for the "Object" Through Standing Like a Tree — 125

1. Categorizing of the "Object" — 125

2. Tao method — 130

3. Method of medicine — 132

4. The Confucius method — 135

5. Taoism and Buddhism Methods — 138

6. Difference between Standing Like a Tree and Qi Gong (Qi practice) — 140

7. The Development of Standing Like a Tree in Modern Times — 142

# Chapter IX : The "Object", or The Second Voluntary Movement — 147

1. Categories of Movement — 147
   - Standards of movement — 149
   - System of movement — 150
   - Process of movement — 150
   - Sole contraction — 150
   - Sole rapid contraction — 151
   - Simultaneous contraction — 151
   - Permanent contraction of the muscles at work + Rapid contraction of the muscles at rest (See drawing below) — 152
   - Permanent contraction of muscles at work + Slow contraction of muscles at rest (see drawing below) — 152
   - Permanent contraction of muscles at work + Permanent contraction of muscles at rest (see drawing below) — 152
   - Mechanism of the creation of movement — 153

2. Primary Voluntary Movement — 153

3. Secondary Voluntary Movement — 154

4. Change in heartbeat in secondary voluntary movement — 155
   a. Change in heartbeat in secondary voluntary movement in a seated position — 155

b. Change in heartbeat in secondary voluntary movement
in a standing position 156

5. Series of training in Standing Like a Tree 159

a. Demands of the primary voluntary movement in
Standing Like a Tree 160
b. Demands of the secondary voluntary movement in
Standing Like a Tree 161

6. Application of Standing Like a Tree 163

a. Sports Domain 163
b. Medical and Health Domain 163
c. Training Domain 163
d. Reaction from actions requiring little effort 163
e. Strength Recovery 164
f. Increase in Productivity 164

7. Conclusion 164

a. Immobility is also a movement 164
b. New Category of voluntary movement 164
c. Mental activities 165
d. Exercise of thought 165
e. Small movement — high-level sport 165
f. Moving in immobility 166
g. Regulation of pulse and breathing 166

# PROLOGUE

# PROLOGUE

## THE END OF AN ERA OF SUPERSTITIONS

China enters the twentieth century, and its last dynasty is in turmoil. On the one hand, international pressures are increasing, foreign countries aim to increase their influence on China; on the other hand, popular discontents increase while the house of the "Son of Heaven" falls apart. The end of the last monarchy marks the beginning of a period of civil wars. The turmoil eventually puts a tragic end to the emperor's heavenly power.

## THE TRANSFORMATION OF MARTIAL ARTS

The present concept of *martial arts* appeared recently. The appearance of firearms, dating from the eighteenth century, precipitates the decline of martial arts practiced by the elite in charge of the interests of the ruling class.

The association of martial arts with philosophies and religious doctrines developed during the last two dynasties. Curiously, it is largely the appearance of firearms that promoted this movement.

Under the Qing Dynasty (1616-), hand- and knife-combat became less popular and were considered as a mean to improve one's health or as a spiritual path, i.e. Taoist calisthenics and certain Buddhist practices. Under the late dynasty, many books dealing with martial arts circulated freely. Most of them dealt with "mysticism" and proclaimed that Zhang San Feng or Bodhidharma were the fathers of most martial arts schools. Stories in which the spirits of these characters protected schools members to the point of immunizing them against firearms ran rampant. Thus, martial arts became a national symbol that was under heavenly protection.

The Rebellion of the Boxers, in the early twentieth century reflected the ideology.

Just as much, the Society of Fists for "justice and harmony" called *the Boxers* by the British, was a secret society founded on the north coast of Shandong. Their members were, for most, farmers and peasants deprived from their land by floods. In despair, they mostly held opium trade, European colonizers and Christian missionaries responsible for their situation. The Boxers believed themselves to be invested with supernatural powers derived from martial arts and calisthenics practices. Pretending to be invulnerable to guns, bullets and Western weaponry and armed with rifles and swords, the Boxers fought against "white evil". It was believed that millions of warrior spirits descended from heaven during the battle to help cleanse China from foreign invaders.

On June 16th, 1900, the widow Empress Ci Xi, called a hearing with the senior officers to decide whether the empire should support or suppress the Boxers. Some officers were skeptical about the veracity and efficiency of their self-proclaimed "supernatural powers", to which the Empress replied:

"Perhaps, we do not have to rely on their magic to defeat the enemy... However, can we deny the faith and spirit of these warriors? Today, China is weak. What is left standing between the colonizers and the Empire is faith. If we do not support this movement and lose hope, who will help the country?"

REINTERPRETATION OF ART IN REPUBLICAN CHINA: THE GUO SHU ERA

During the Republican period up until 1947, martial artists promoted their art with a deep military mindset. After 1947, the vision and use of martial changed to become simpler and more efficient.

## CENTRAL NATIONAL ACADEMY OF ARTS OF NANJING

The Guan Zhong Yang Guo Shu was developed during the Republican period to promote *Kung Fu*. During this period, the purpose of practicing martial arts was to eradicate superstition, give up its aesthetics aspect, unnecessary elements, redefine the essential, and deepen roots. This era was called Guo Shu or "National Art."

### WANG XIANGZHAI

Wang Xiangzhai (1885-1963) embodies the spirit of this reform, which was materialized into what was called *internal art*. It redefined the relationship between movement and stillness, were stillness took over from movement. Following a long journey through China in search of the ancient roots of martial arts, Master Wang developed a new training system called *Yi Quan*. The new system reinstated the practice of Zhan Zhuang [phonetic pronunciation: Djan Djuang] (lit. Pillar Practice, Standing Like a Tree). It became the new training's central axis. Moreover, it put an end to the old system and traditional routines and strongly condemns the semi-slavery-like traditional relationship between master and disciples. It promoted a more natural relationship whereby the teacher and the disciple were on a same level. "Knowledge should not be mysterious or subject to speculations and manipulation, but rather openly disclosed and discussed without reservation, all for the good of humanity."

### THE PEOPLE'S REPUBLIC OF CHINA: THE WU SHU OF SPORTS AND HEALTH

After the defeat of Japan, the civil war between Guo Ming Tang and Tang Gong Chang (Communist Party) was revived. On October 1st, 1945, Mao Zedong proclaimed China's first People's Republic. To the world of martial arts, it had a profound impact. Under this new regime, most critics argue that the new forms lost their original energetic spirits to become purely aesthetic disciplines.

Martial arts then took two different directions: health, and competition. Tai Chi [phonetic pronunciation: tai tchee], stripped of its *internal* and martial aspect, became part of a campaign to strengthen national health. *Wu Shu* (lit. Martial Arts) and the *Sanda* were considered as a sports and were sought to be integrated as Olympic disciplines.

## THE RESEARCH ASSOCIATION OF CHINESE KUNG FU IN PEKING: ZHONG GUO QUAN XUE XIE HUI

Under the People's Republic of China, as "comrades shouldn't fight amongst themselves", martial arts were banned in public places, which forced Wang Xiangzhai and his students to change the purpose of their art into a healing practice. They subsequently founded the Association for Research on Chinese Kung Fu, which perpetuated the revisionist spirit of the previous era. Determined to preserve martial arts and at a time when the practice was doomed to disappear, Wang Xiangzhai worked underground towards enriching it by bringing the latest discoveries in biodynamic, reflex conduct and new evolutionary theories that appeared in China at the time.

## YU YONGNIAN 于永年: THE ART OF INTENTION

Yu Yongnian was born under the People's Republic of China regime. He studied at Harbin, and during his years in Japan obtained a graduate degree in 1941 at the University of Odontology in Tokyo.

He began his practice in Beijing, at the Train Hospital. After long years of study Dr. Yu Yongnian was physically worn out. He decided to practice Tai Chi. At the time in Beijing, many people were speaking of Wang Xiangzhai. His appearances in the press and rumors of his unusual talents aroused Yu Yongnian's curiosity. In 1944 he began training with Master Wang.

The core's training was to stand as still as a statue for an extended period of time, i.e. Zhan Zhuang. That process challenged the very core of Yu's understanding of martial arts, which caused him to give up training on several occasions. In 1949, after the proclamation of the People's Republic of China, Master Wang changed his training methods towards prevention and treatment of disease. As such, many patients began to practice Zhan Zhuang. The number of patients kept increasing.

Dr. Yu witnessed unusual quick recoveries. Deeply impressed, he brought Zhan Zhuang as an experimental treatment to the hospital where he worked. Results were surprising. Dr. Yu could not comprehend how staying in one position could cure serious illnesses. The young Dr. Yu took this fact as an intellectual challenge, which drove him to study in depth the physiological mechanism by which these *miracles* occurred.

> *... There is no reason to blindly believe old superstitions. Today, we have very useful tools to understand internal mechanisms and discriminate the real from the unreal...*

There was yet another challenge: understanding the origin of the *internal force* from a scientific and rational standpoint. Dr. Yu studied in depth Classical Chinese texts as well theories from Einstein, Darwin, Pavlov, among others.

> *If we associate the theory of relativity of Einstein and the theory of evolution of species, we obtain the* Tao De Jing *of Laozi.*

The result of Dr. Yu's search eventually materialized into a unique art, Zhan Zhuang, an art that combines physical as well as mental trainings.

> *The road to recovery leads to obtaining the* Wu. *The* Wu *is the vector of consciousness. One perceives* Tao De Jing *very differently when one has the* Wu...

The art of nourishing life through Zhan Zhuang allows us to discover the common denominator of all *internal* arts. It leads to the development of *Nei Jin* (internal force), called *Wu* (Substance).

*We now know that there is a concrete path to reach the inner strength, which is what we call "voluntary exercises of the second type."*
*The link between the mind and body exists in within us.*
*This ends the duality which was called "Returning to the Tao, or merging with the One."*

Karim Nimri

# INTERVIEW WITH DR. YU YONGNIAN

# INTERVIEW WITH DR. YU YONGNIAN

## THE POWER OF PEACE

◉ Professor Yu, why have you started practicing martial arts? From what I read, after finishing medical school, your physical condition deteriorated. Is that why you started practicing?

Initially I studied Tai Chi and Xing Yi Quan. Around 1944, I had already completed my medical studies and I was already working in the dentistry department at the hospital. It is true that my health was not very good; during the winter, I would catch a cold easily, and in the spring it would not improve much. For one reason or another, I would always catch something...

◉ And why choose Tai Chi or *internal* martial arts?

In China, in the medical field, there is the idea that people who exercise regularly and develop their body, muscles, will inevitably cause their circulatory system to deteriorate. The heart and blood circulation will be affected by excess, leading to a shortening of life. However, when someone assiduously practises gentle and slow exercises, their circulatory system strengthens and lengthens their lives, which is why people that practice Tai Chi tend to live longer. If we think of the animal kingdom, the lion or the tiger possess spectacular strength, but their life expectancy is rather short. However, the elephant and the tortoise, animals which move rather slowly, live over a hundred years.

And if we compare the animal and vegetable kingdoms: How many years can a tree live? In Beijing's parks, there are many ancient trees, gigantic cypress that are over a thousand years old. In Australia, there are sequoias over ten thousand years old. In Chinese, they have a very interesting name, *shi yoyo*, which means "grandfather of the world". To return to the topic of sports, the majority of people do not understand, think that the more they move, the better it is; the higher the speed, the better it is. Like running the marathon and that sort of things. However, in China, from antiquity to the present day, it is a question whether the best exercise is to move or stand still, a subject that is still being debated today, the conflict between movement and stillness. Initially, I also understood that but later I found the answer in the *Tao De Jing*, which solves the dilemma. Do you know what I mean?

☙ I think so, is it *Bao yi duli bu kai* (embrace the one alone and without changing)?

Almost. *Bao yi wu li kai* (or also : embrace the one, without abandoning nor going away). Embracing the one is easy, anyone can do it. But persevering, staying this way for forty minutes, an hour, it's more difficult. However, the longer one practises, the more the internal changes and the greater the transformation. This is not to say that peace is the only way. Training in motion, that is to say, Tai Chi, has also many health benefits.

☙ Tai Chi through movement is therefore the same as Zhan Zhuang through peace?

When one practices *Gong Fu*, one plays with *Jin* or *Wu*. All look the same. The thing we need to keep in mind is the method that brings us the closest to the objective; we must stress on that which makes us progress the most, either through movement or stillness. From my perspective, what will bring us the greatest experience of the Jin force lies in the motionless practice, but as we said, it is a debate that dates back to antiquity. For most people, exercise involves movement. However, training the internal by an outer immobility is a practice that produces surprising results, although it is hard for some to believe.

That said, it is necessary to practice for a long time. Moreover, if nobody tells us what to look for or how to find it, it is very difficult to persevere. One must have great confidence in one's teacher to overcome these barriers.

◉ Furthermore, reading ancient texts on Kung Fu, information is often very vague and very difficult to understand, especially for Westerners. Perhaps this leaves too much room for speculation?

It is difficult to find a theoretical information that is precise, useful, and explained with verifiable scientific parameters. The theory of Kung Fu which we inherited from our ancestors reflects the reality of the time, the information was codified and too abstract, so the theory was not easy to understand if you do not have not someone to explain it to you.

But today, we rediscover ancient knowledge with the means provided by modern science. Results are in a verifiable form. We understand better ancient concepts. We should not train on blind faith alone, solely based on information from a remote past. For example, we speak of "finding stillness in movement of Tai Chi and movement in stillness with Qi Gong [*tchee gong* in phonetic pronunciation]" How do we measure the movement in stillness? How is it verifiable?

◉ I do not know. Is there a means to measure the movement in stillness?

There is one, but until recently, no one knew how to measure it.

In fact, it is enough to just measure one's pulse to see that with practice of a static posture, without moving, the pulse can rise up to 150 beats. This is an example of what we were talking about.

☻ You mean, with the pulse, it is possible to determine the degree of internal movement?

Yes, of course. It is not an external movement, but an internal one. If it moves very, very slowly, it is possible that the heart rate does not change, and yet without moving, it can go over 150.

☻ With such rapid heart rate, there would be some respiratory problems, breathing wouldn't be normal...

You see? That's the advantage. In any sport, with a heart rate above 100, one begins to pant. But with the practice of Zhan Zhuang, at a faster pace, you get you out of breath. There are physical activities that cause us to lose oxygen in the blood, and others where oxygen is not lost, but where it accumulates. That is why, when one practises Zhan Zhuang for over twenty minutes, even if one begins to sweat, the mind is more clear and the breathing does not accelerate.

☻ Can you tell us about your meeting with Wang Xiangzhai and give us your first impression?

He was an elderly man, neither fat nor thin, neither tall nor short, with a little belly. A normal man for his age. He must have been about fifty or could have very well been in his sixties. I was 23 or 24. He was very bright, healthy, but he did not look like someone practising Kung Fu. You know, people who practice *Wu Shu* are generally stocky, with lots of muscles (laughs). He looked more like an educated person. His attitude was not that of a fighter, but that of a scholar.

☯ Basically if you had bumped into him on a street, you would have never imagined he practiced Wu Shu...

No, he didn't seem like that, but his physical condition was admirable, and his gait was very sharp and swift. We, at twenty, were unable to follow. I admit that at first I could not believe it... I thought: "By practicing only Zhan Zhuang, standing doing nothing, can we develop inner strength?" Besides, he did not look particularly special, he was a normal man, he didn't seem to possess exceptional abilities. I had only heard what others said about his dexterity... Knowing I was a doctor, and it was said he had the ability to cure diseases, I could hardly believe it. So I had my doubts. But with time, I realized that my teacher was right, and the results had convinced me.

☯ Where were you training with him?

We trained in Tai Miao, the current Palace of the culture of workers, on the east side of Tian'an men Square. In the morning, many people came to train; over a hundred. It is at this point that I started to train with them.

The real beginning was in Beijing between 1942 and 1944 at Pichai Hutong, in Xidan, under the Japanese occupation. It was after the seizure of Japan in 1945 that they began practicing Tai Miao. That's when I joined the group. After the Liberation (1947), the classes were moved to the Zhong Shan Park.

☯ From what I know, in the early days of the Wang Xiangzhai teaching, students mainly practiced fighting, was it not?

Exactly. At the beginning, he taught us boxing. The students were very young and enjoyed fighting. It was the era of Yao Zong Xun, who began studying before me. At that time, after having studied for a few years, students sought strong opponents to test their skills.

☯ So it was pure boxing...

Yes, at Pichai Hutong, students were mainly learning how to fight, and, the truth is that Wang Xiang's students Zhai fought against opponents who practiced other styles, and they usually proved themselves stronger. But it is true that many of them were only preoccupied with fighting, and some even abused their power. The overall impression was not very positive. People thought we practiced Da Cheng Quan [phonetic pronunciation: da tcheng tchuan], and that we were fighters, troublemakers. So, the reputation we had was not positive, of course.

Over the years, this was the reason why Yao Zong Xun gave up its name to go back to the original style and was so renamed Yi Quan, hoping to get rid of the bad reputation that followed Da Cheng Quan. That is why, in the Yao Zong Xun's training system, it is still called Yi Quan.

☯ But then, what is the correct name, Yi Quan or Da Cheng Quan?

Yi Quan is the name of the style developed by Wang Xiangzhai in Shanghai during his time, that is to say, the time before his arrival in Beijing. The system began to be called Da Cheng Quan during the Beijing's era. But it was not the idea of Wang himself, but of his disciples.

Da Cheng is a Confucian concept indicating a very high degree of personal development, among scholars. Da Cheng Quan means "boxing through great achievement." Yi Quan derives from Xing Yi Quan (boxing through form and intent), but Xing was withdrawn because Xing Yi Quan does not have forms nor routines.

Zhang Bi Hua gave the name Da Cheng and Wang Xiangzhai initially agreed. However, he thought that the knowledge of the man was unlimited, as the knowledge of martial arts, and to call it "great achievement" could give a wrong idea about that of unlimited knowledge.

The two names correspond to different eras. The Yi Quan era dates back in the 1920s in Shanghai, Da Cheng Quan dates back to Beijing during the 1940s. Eventually, it was given the final name of Xue Zhong Guo Quan or "science of Chinese boxing" or "Chinese Kung Fu".

  We can say that these three designations correspond to three different periods, does it not? But "the science of Chinese boxing" is a more general name...

The science of Chinese boxing is the result of many years of research on the foundations, the pillars of the practice of Chinese Kung Fu. Otherwise, if you want to call it the first era of Da Cheng Quan or Yi Quan, it really does not matter. But the name that corresponds to the last era is Zhong Guo Quan Xue Yan Jiu Hui (association of the research on Chinese Kung Fu or Chinese boxing).

The inscription on the tomb of Wang Xiangzhai, Xue Yan Jiu Hui Yi Quan (Yi Quan Research Association) is incorrect, because the final stage was to move from one style of fighting or boxing to investigate the science of martial arts. Such has been its evolution, this is the reality.

  And how does such a martial style develop into a science of culture and of health, of Yang Sheng?

After the Liberation, the practice of martial arts was banned.

And although there were many people interested in martial arts like Yao Zong Xun and Wang Jie Xuan, we were very interested in Zhan Zhuang. It was not only the therapeutic side of it, but also its means to preserve health, *Yang Sheng*. I was a doctor, I could not pick a fight over there (laughs), and I was interested more in investigation and studying in depth the aspect of prevention and treatment of diseases.

๏ So how does this research group, interested in the therapeutic aspect of Zhan Zhuang, investigated it? By reading books?

At that time there were no books, nor any material available. There were ancient Buddhist and Taoist texts, but no recent and more precise publications. References to the practice in the ancient books were very vague. And recent publications were small booklets that barely taught postures, nothing more, nothing concrete.

๏ In June 1981, Zhan Zhuang Jian Shen Liang Fa (Zhan Zhuang a good method for health), the first book on Zhan Zhuang teaching techniques to promote health was published. The first edition sold 120,000 copies, and the second more than 275,000.

Yes, it was in general a theoretical explanation of Zhan Zhuang. It also included some medical cases, but nothing more. It is in later publications that medical records were included.

๏ I understand that the application of Zhan Zhuang in hospitals began in the 1950s Apparently Wang Xiangzhai was invited to hospitals and clinics across China to teach Zhan Zhuang as a therapy. When did he begin treating patients with Zhan Zhuang? What was his approach?

After the Liberation, in 1947, coinciding with the period of

Tai Miao, many people went to local parks to cure their health problems. Essentially, we practiced Zhan Zhuang, but when the sick and the weak left we continued with Tui Shou, pushing with hands.

☯ I understand that this change came from the prohibition by the government of the martial arts, and Wang Xiangzhai then concentrated his practice on the treatment of disease.

Yes, that's right, and very successfully. As I said, many people came for this reason, with health problems such as arthritis or an affected shoulder that did not allow them to raise an arm, people coming in wheelchairs pushed by their family… These people, after half a month or a month were recovering mobility and started to walk alone. At that time, I saw patients that did not improve their health a bit while in the hospital but did were in the park, almost immediately. It was then, in the physiotherapy section of the hospital, we created a new department called "exercises for recovery" (Ti Liao ke).

At first there were not many patients, but the department soon began to fill up. On the fifth floor of the hospital of western medicine, we had a huge room where we practiced Zhan Zhuang in the morning. Despite the skepticism, word of mouth worked well and, in no time, we welcomed many people.

☯ And what happened to martial practice, did it disappear?

At Tai Miao, most were practicing Zhan Zhuang for health, but there was also a group that was training at Yao Zong Xun's home, in Xidan. They were all young students learning combat but clandestinely, because it was not allowed. This did not mean there was a change in the ways of Wang Xiangzhai. The number of people practicing Yang Sheng (for health) was growing and the number who trained for combat was shrinking, and so, the practice evolved towards the prevention and cure of diseases. Anyways, the therapeutic results were very good.

☯ What types of diseases were treated?

All chronic illnesses: hypertension, arthritis, coronary heart diseases, digestion, insomnia... Insomnia has given excellent results.

☯ What was the reaction of the medical community?

There was no concrete feedback. At first just occupied a rehabilitation room at the general hospital of Peking. Other hospitals did not have such courses, but they gradually began to include similar activities, but used only the generic name *Qi Gong*.

☯ How did the Zhan Zhuang therapy and Qi Gong differ?

At first they were very similar. We all practiced with static postures, standing, sitting or lying down. After creating the sanatorium of Beidahe, they started calling it Qi Gong, and the Chinese medicine hospitals also called it Qi Gong and not Zhan Zhuang. In 1967, they invited Wang Xiangzhai to the Research Institute of Chinese medicine and created the Department of Research on Qi Gong. It was called Qi Gong but Zhan Zhuang was practiced like in the hospital of Guan'an men or the one in Baoding.

☯ So initially, the practice was the same, but with different names? Because they followed different paths thereafter...

It's exactly that. In the 1960s at Xiao Tang Shan, a seminar was held where all sanatoria and rehabilitation services in the country spoke of Zhan Zhuang. Then I went to Shanghai where we also presented it ; the from was accepted in all these institutions as a therapy, but it was called Qi Gong because the name already had a reputation and Zhan Zhuang did not.

Then came the Qi Gong *boom* and many systems emerged thereafter ; some were positive and some much less so. Like those who practice Fa Gon, who emit Qi with their hands and change the composition of the water, or who tell you they are sending Qi from Beijing to a patient in Hong Kong and healing him... (laughs). All this is false... It started about forty years ago.

And suddenly it became very funny, because if you said it was wrong, nobody believed it, everyone was very excited about it. Then Li Hong Zhi appeared and created Fa Lun Gong. He also taught on the basis of Zhan Zhuang, but added things like "Fa Lun Wheel" orbits etc. They promised spectacular things. But it ended in a tragedy.

The first steps of the Qi Gong therapy are very positive and very useful from a therapeutic point of view. The problem is with higher steps, such as "open the gate of heaven", micro-orbit, macro-orbit... These elements can cause problems. By practicing Qi Gong, the focus is on the middle line in the meridian system, while in the practice of Zhan Zhuang, one practices on the four members of the body. It is best not to focus on the centre and not to control the breathing. Natural breathing is the best, for then the brain is able to relax. The extremities are the most important, this is where we concentrate our work, thanks to them, we connect with our internal centres (bodies) and we develop our capacity, our potentiality. The lower extremities are even more important, the potential is much greater. Today, men are putting great emphasis on the movements of upper limbs, but there is much more potential in the legs.

☯ Did you know the original therapy of Qi Gong? What was it?

In ancient times, there were methods of Yang Sheng, the culture of health, used by people of high intellectual and culture. In my view, this whole culture of Yang Sheng comes mainly from Tao De Jing of Laozi. A very important part of the Tao De Jing is to cultivate life or health. Understanding this is very important.

☯ And the Buddhist contribution?

In Buddhism, the main one is the sitting posture. The Chinese cultural tradition brings this little gem that is standing meditation, sometimes with a martial vocation, but always centered on the development of global energy and integrated in the center.

☯ But the training system which, according to tradition, brought the Bodhidharma in Shao Lin also includes standing postures.

Yes, it is true, but the first references to standing meditation existed in the Chinese culture a thousand years earlier than it did in the "Classic of the Yellow Emperor" and especially in the Tao De Jing.

Thereafter, the only practice of Zhan Zhuang, which had perhaps become too difficult and too elementary, evolved towards a practice in movement, then came those who were called internal martial arts. These styles are based on movement, and Qi Gong, on peace.

☯ What is the future of Zhan Zhuang as a therapy today?

Zhan Zhuang therapy is currently used in very few places. In the medical field, we still use a lot of acupuncture and Tuina massage, but static practices are in decline.

☯ Can we get it back to it?

It is now at the stage in which it was a few years ago. In hospitals, we can say that this practice has almost disappeared. Today, the practice is done on a personal level, at home, in some schools, in public parks with professors. Surely, it does not benefit from the fame it had a years ago.

☯ Who do you think Zhan Zhuang could benefit to?

We should spread and promote this practice to the ones affected with chronic diseases that cannot be cured with medication. Zhan Zhuang can rebalance health effectively and without resorting to aggressive treatments.

There has been an increasing level of interest, especially abroad. In China, considering what happened to Fa Lun Gong practitioners, Zhang Zhuang is a subject that is avoided. Da Cheng Quan practice has been greatly affected by all that. However, we must not lose hope in Zhan Zhuang, which is more than a therapy or a art for combat, it is also one of the best ways to prevent disease, an extraordinary method for preserving and reinforcing health.

Karim Nimri

# ZHAN ZHUAN
## THE ART OF NOURISHING LIFE

# CHAPTER I
# INTRODUCTION

## 1. MEDICAL EFFECTS OF STANDING LIKE A TREE

A tree, although still, is alive and grows continuously until it becomes strong and solid. Perhaps inspired by this phenomenon of nature, our ancestors invented this method of training called *Standing Like a Tree*.

Today, Standing Like a Tree is not only a basic exercise for practicing martial arts but also an exercise that has medical benefits.

According to our first few experiments, this method provides efficient results for healing chronic diseases such as tracheitis, gastroenteritis, hepatitis, heart disease, hypertension, neurasthenia, rheumatoid arthritis and diseases similar to the latter and as well as those associated with fatty tissues (lipoma), swelling of the thyroid gland etc.

The most important characteristic from a medical point of view is its absence of side effects. To practice Standing Like a Tree, it is not necessary to be absolutely calm nor artificially regulate your breathing. Neither is there a need to focus on the Dan Tian (stomach's energy center) nor master the primary and secondary Meridian Circulation. You can practice this in an area that is sunny and full of fresh air, indoors or outdoors, by positioning yourself correctly, holding yourself as still as a tree trunk and breathing naturally so that the body can be both relaxed without being loose and tight without being stiff. There are several simple ways to practice Standing Like a Tree. The duration of the exercise can be modified and can vary from five minutes to an hour. Anyone can do it anywhere, at any time but according to one's physical fitness.

We know that each one of us has the capacity to protect himself against attacks from the outside, for example from viruses or bacteria, by creating antibodies. However, this ability differs from person to person depending on the place and time. When the antibody production occurs too slowly, there is a risk of the germs penetrating the wound; and once in the body they can easily proliferate and destroy the immune system. However, if the reaction is quick, it can efficiently protect the body and keep it in good health.

The reason why practicing Standing Like a Tree can cure a disease and strengthen the body is linked to the fact that during this particular exercise the body's ability to protect itself is reinforced by improving the regulatory system. As the exercise requires the bending of your arms and legs to a certain level, this means that the muscles must constantly stretch and contract to support the body frame. Consequently, it increases the blood circulation, the quantity of which increases considerably due to the movement of blood that was stagnant in the organs. At the same time, the capillary vessels in the muscles dilate which results in a feeling of pins and needles in the arms and legs, tingling sensation under the skin and perspiration with the feeling of heat in the body.

Normally, a blood analysis carried out before and after the daily, regular exercise of one hour shows an increase in red cells, white cells and hemoglobin, of around 1 520 000 units, 3 650 units and 3.2 grams by mm$^3$ respectively. Hemoglobin transports oxygen throughout the body. When it passes through the lungs it releases carbon dioxide and absorbs 96% of the oxygen which it then distributes by passing through the other organs permitting them to function properly. The amount of oxygen in the blood is proportional to the volume of hemoglobin present in the body. An increase of the former leads to an increase in the latter, bringing around the strange sensation of relaxation and well-being and strengthening of the cerebral cortex benefits. This is why the practice of Standing Like a Tree is efficient against diseases such as asthenia, arthritis, angina, arteriosclerosis etc.

Disorders such as headaches, insomnia and sleeping problems are symptoms of asthenia or major chronic diseases for which doctors do not have many effective solutions. The phenomenon of sleep is a process of control that is carried out in the middle and below the cerebral cortex. It is difficult to fall asleep and to have many dreams if the degree of control is not sufficient. People suffering from headaches and lacking vitality due to insomnia can be healed by Standing Like a Tree exercise if taking medication does not help. After more than 30-40 minutes of training, the improvement in blood circulation and metabolic processes eliminates the symptoms of headaches and the lack of vitality. At the same time, you experience a pleasant feeling in the head and chest that cannot be accurately described.

Some patients who experience heavy-headedness before the exercise feel as light as a swallow in flight afterwards. The longer the duration, the more significant the effect. All of this is the result of the training that allows quick control of the nervous system.

The traditional medical profession does not recommend the practice of sports to the people suffering from heart or circulatory problems because of the aggressive movements which bring about side effects such as the acceleration of the heart rate and breathing difficulties which are difficult to control. Practicing Standing Like a Tree does not involve these kinds of constraints and offers a proper mastery of the movement created by the different postures and therefore, can specially cure heart diseases.

During the exercise, working the two hands in a "pull/hold" position reduces the natural pressure that the shoulders exert on the lungs, which in turn increases the lung capacity. Throughout the exercise, we notice that the amplitude of muscular movements is growing, creating natural breathing in the stomach. This form of natural breathing without any side effects can massage the stomach, cure constipation and improve digestion and absorption functions. Consequently, the patients' level of fitness quickly improves until they are fully healed. Thin people gain weight and obese ones lose.

The lack of physical exercise leads to an anticipated deterioration of physiological functioning. Practicing Standing Like a Tree for a long period of time allows us to remain relatively younger than people of the same age. Generally, adults lose about 1% of their heart's ability to supply blood. At 60, the speed of the blood flow in the limbs is 30-40% slower than in a young man'. The muscles in the chest equally harden because of the lack of movement for so many years. This reduces more and more the volume of one inhalation. At 70, the nervous system's speed of communication drops by 10-15%. Of course, the deterioration of these functions with age can be slowed down by practicing suitable sports regularly. This deterioration brings about a decrease in heart rate for elderly people in a normal state of health and doing sport increases the blood flow with every pulsation. Permanent exercise also improves the circulatory and respiratory system and reinforces muscular contraction ability. This facilitates the protection of joints against accidents and hardening with time. Since the percentage of calcium increases after exercise, the risks of fractures are reduced.

## 2. REACTIONS AFTER STANDING LIKE A TREE

During the course of the exercise of Standing like a Tree, you can observe several reactions due to modifications in the internal functioning of the body:

### A. SENSATIONS OF PINS AND NEEDLES AND ACHES

It appears at the beginning of the training. We quickly grow accustomed to this little discomfort. It gradually goes from the fingers to the feet, the legs, shoulders, back and so on and so forth. We feel as though an ant or a little insect is walking on the skin without being able to precisely locate it. This phenomenon, directly linked to Standing Like a Tree, is caused because of the dilation of the capillary blood vessels which facilitates an acceleration in blood circulation.

## B. FEELING OF PAINFUL SWELLING

During the first weeks of training, participants feel a painful swelling and fatigue in certain areas of the leg, knee, side, shoulder, neck etc. It should be noted that the reactions listed above are physiological and normal after exercising. They disappear after a few weeks. In areas where there are old wounds or operations sudden pains may occur. This is a normal reaction due to old traumas. Another type of reaction arises in affected areas, for example, headaches for people affected by asthenia, stomach aches for those who have bowel or stomach problems, joint pain for those suffering from arthritis, stinging sensations behind the neck for those with thyroid problems etc.

This positive phenomenon, which can disappear after 3 to 10 days, represents an important change taking place in the body; indicating great improvement in the functioning of the metabolism.

## C. FEELING OF HEAT

During each session, after 20 minutes of exercising, you begin to feel hot and to sweat. The more the duration and degree of bending, the more abundant the perspiration becomes. It feels great to get to this stage of perspiration as it spreads a feeling of lightness and relaxation all over the body.

The exercise also has reactions such as hiccups and winds. Sometimes, loud noises can be heard from the stomach.

## D. FEELING OF VIBRATIONS

A solid position requires a good hold of compressed strength by the limbs of the body. Exercising the muscles this much makes them begin to tremble. At the beginning, this phenomenon is light and short and can be observed by touching the sensitive parts of the knee, leg etc. Gradually, it gets stronger and stronger and the constant rhythmic wobbling is felt in the muscle and in the inner and outer parts of the leg. The vibration then further increases and we get to the stage where the phenomenon of twitching can be observed. After some time, the resistance to fatigue and the ability to control the nervous system are reinforced. Then step by step, the opposite way is experienced going from the phenomenon of twitching to trembling or a complete stand still.

## E. FEELING OF DIFFERENCE

The main feelings of difference during the training are the following:

- Difference of height:

During the exercise it can often happen that the left and right hand are not at the same level while we strongly believe that they are and vice-versa; when both hands are at the same level, we believe that they are not. This is due to the imbalance of physical development and strength usually used on each side of our body.

- Difference of pins and needles:

You may feel a sensation of pins and needles on only one side of the body and not on the other. The same applies to a headache which can be present on one side and not on the other. This phenomenon is more predominant for those suffering from hypertension.

- Difference in perspiration:

Because of the deregulation of the autonomic nervous system some of the participants only perspire on one side of the body, for example, only the right-hand side of the face or the head is covered in heavy perspiration whereas there is none on the left-hand side. This phenomenon, for which conventional doctors are unable to find the cause, is purely observed on the line of separation between the left and the right sides.

- Difference in the circulatory system:

This happens to some after around 20 minutes of training. After having maintained an equal load on the body by keeping the two arms at the same height, a difference is observed between them; one is normal and the other is contracted, stiff with the skin appearing dark-red. This comes with a feeling of heaviness and a sensation ofpins and needles in the fingers up to the shoulders only on that particular arm.

- Difference in temperature:

This phenomenon is mostly pronounced in the hand: for example, to have a warm feeling in the right hand and a cold feeling in the left. The difference in temperature measured by placing a probe between the fingers was 10 degrees maximum. Some participants even notice a difference in temperature between the 5 fingers.

The phenomenon of differences listed above may reduce in certain participants after 2 or 3 weeks of training and can even disappear after 2 or 3 months. On the other hand, other people may never be able to make it disappear completely.

F. FEELING OF WELL-BEING AND JOY

After a certain period of time spent in exercising, the control in the inside of the brain is strengthened, the metabolism, the circulatory system as well as other physical functions of the body are improved. There is a sort of exceptional feeling of well being and joy. It settles in the body and the head becomes clear, the stomach and chest are light and free, the symptoms of the illnesses are gone, the mind is in high spirits, the four limbs are full of energy and all the parts of the body are in state of complete liberty. This sensation of well being is reinforced gradually with practice.

The medical effects produced by practicing Standing Like a Tree during the first weeks are presented in list I.

It is acknowledged that aches and the feeling of pins and needles, which are predominant during the first two weeks, progressively reduce from the 3rd week onwards. Also, the feeling of joy and well being, which does not usually manifest for the first 2 or 3 weeks, is felt little by little after 3 or 4 weeks of training. The longer the duration, the more significant the effect is. From the 6th week onward, give or take a few days depending on the people, it is recommended to increase the intensity of the exercise so that the aches and the sensation of pins and needles reappear. This cycle of reactions should be regularly regulated by the control of the intensity of practice. It allows the body to be strong and cures diseases.

## 3. PRECAUTIONS TO TAKE DURING THE TRAINING

1. Go to the bathroom before exercising so as not to be interrupted.
2. Unbutton your collar, loosen your belt, take off your watch and untie your shoelaces so that the entire body can be in a complete state of freedom.
3. For beginners as well as people having a more or less weak level of fitness, practice without closing your eyes in the beginning. If after 20 minutes of exercising the sensation of well-being manifests, you can close your eyes. If this causes a headache that brings about a feeling of instability, they may be left open to help maintain the body's balance.
4. The mouth is to remain in a natural position, neither too closed nor too open, with a bit of space between the lips and teeth.
5. The aim of the medical practice of Standing Like a Tree consists in keeping a fixed position and observing the changes on the inside of the body. People who have difficulties in concentrating can count their breaths. Breathing should be natural without trying to accelerate it, neither consciously prolonging

its duration nor holding your breath.
6. It is preferable to perform the exercise with your back turned towards the sun, avoiding bright light that bothers the eyes. It is quite a pleasant experience to let the sun heat up the back during the exercise, especially during winter and autumn.
7. When the exercise is being done in a room, it is better to have a calm surrounding, fresh air and a suitable temperature.
8. Try to control yourself by reducing the swaying caused by trembling of the muscles of the legs.
9. When the exercise is over, gradually reduce the movement by slowly straightening your legs and lowering your arms. Before leaving your spot cross your hands behind your back, relax for 2 to 3 minutes while waiting for the sensations of aches and pins and needles to disappear.
10. For people who have difficulties in sleeping and wish to practice Standing Like a Tree before going to bed, there are two possible ways depending on the type of your nervous system:
    - Controlled type: The participants are able sleep right after the exercise. In this case, it is recommended to do the exercise right before sleeping.
    - Type that becomes hyper after training: In this case, it is recommended to do the exercise 2 or 3 hours before going to bed, leaving 1 or 2 hours of resting time.
11. The exercise is to be done half an hour before or after eating so as not to disturb the digestion.
12. Female participants who have their menstrual cycle can continue the exercise provided that its side effects do not disturb the body too much. At the very least, it is recommended to reduce the intensity of the exercise to rest better. The complete exercise can be carried out again after the menstrual cycle is over.

| Type | Reactions | 1st week | 2nd week | 3rd week | 4th week | 5th week | 6th week |
|---|---|---|---|---|---|---|---|
| Pins and needles | • Hands | + | + | ++ | ++ | + | - |
| | • Feet | + | + | ++ | ++ | + | - |
| | • Head | - | - | - | ± | ± | ± |
| | • Chest | - | - | - | ± | ± | ± |
| | • Body | - | - | - | - | ± | ± |
| | • Tingling | - | ± | ± | + | + | + |
| Aches | • Shoulder | + | ++ | + | ± | - | - |
| | • Neck | - | - | + | ++ | + | - |
| | • Knee | + | ++ | ++ | + | ± | - |
| | • Leg | + | ++ | + | - | - | - |
| | • Back & Sides | - | ± | ± | - | - | - |
| | • Wound | - | ± | + | - | - | - |
| | • Diseased area | - | - | ± | + | - | - |
| Rise in temperature | • Hiccough | ± | + | + | + | ± | ± |
| | • Fart | ± | + | + | + | ± | ± |
| | • Growling in the stomach | - | - | - | ± | ± | ± |
| | • Heat | ± | + | + | + | - | - |
| | • Perspiration | ± | + | + | + | ± | - |
| Trembling | • Trembling | - | + | + | + | - | - |
| | • Heartbeats | - | - | + | + | - | - |
| | • Twitching | - | - | - | + | + | - |
| Difference | • Height of arms | + | + | + | + | + | + |
| | • Length of legs | - | - | + | + | + | + |
| | • Pins and needles in the sides | - | - | - | ± | ± | ± |
| | • Perspiration on both the sides | - | - | ± | ± | + | + |
| | • Circulation on both the sides | - | - | - | ± | ± | + |
| | • Temperature on on both sides | - | - | ± | ± | + | - |
| Well-being (Euphoria) Joy | • Light-headedness | - | - | + | + | ++ | +++ |
| | • Relaxed chest | - | - | + | + | ++ | +++ |
| | • Cheerfulness | - | - | + | + | ++ | +++ |

Medical effects and reactions produced by the practice of Standing Like a Tree during the first weeks

Notes:
 "+": Present
 "-": Absent
 "±": Present or Absent
 "++": Strong
 "+++": Very strong

# CHAPTER II
# UPRIGHT POSITION

## 1. DIFFERENT POSITIONS IN STANDING LIKE A TREE

Several types of positions can be used to practise Standing like a Tree: lying down flat, seated, standing and walking. Amongst these different positions, the most used and efficient one is the standing position, which is why it has been named, "Standing Like a Tree".

The standing position is a basic exercise for people practising Standing Like a Tree and Da Cheng Quan. It has two main aims; one of which is designed to maintain good health and the other, for the art of combat.

The first use of several standing positions consists in distributing the weight of the body on the legs in a homogenous manner. The intensity of the exercise is set by the flexion of the legs and the height at which the arms are raised. Consequently, depending on the physical fitness of each participant, the adjustment is relatively and thus makes the positions adaptable for the beginners.

The second use, training for combat, is based on a standing position slightly bent in such a way that the distribution of the body weight is not homogeneous. In the beginning, the proportion can be at 40% on the foot in front and 60% on the foot behind and then, at 30% and 70% ratio with training. One exception is the Contra-Step where weight distribution is reversed. This practice is not very suitable for beginners, As the weight distribution is not equal on both the feet.

The principle practice of Standing Like a Tree, meant for health purposes, consists in maintaining the following positions:

- The two feet are apart shoulder width apart

- The two knees are slightly bent
- The body is in a seated position (not necessary for people having a low level of fitness)
- The hands with the palms facing downwards or upwards, slowly rise as though the arms are squeezing something between them.
- The height of the hands vary between that of the eyebrows and the navel. The horizontal position varies between 30 cm in front of the body and a position very close to the stomach without actually touching it. The adjustment in this zone thus avoids pressure on the lungs as well as incorrect breathing caused by inaccurate shoulder and chest positions.
- The degree of flexing of the legs is set in such a way that it is manageable and the pain isn't too unbearable.
- The shoulder muscles, back muscles and chest muscles must all be in a completely relaxed state so that breathing can take place naturally, so that the chest is relaxed, the head feels clear and the body is serene with an equal distribution of strength.

Practising Standing Like a Tree thus consists in holding a position and maintaining it, apparently without moving. It is through this un moving position that we notice the changes inside our body and as well as sensations of aches and pins and needles that appear in the shoulders and legs. One may reduce this reaction by lowering the arms, putting the legs back or by just standing up straight to relax a little.

Beginners can increase the intensity of the exercise by doing 5 to 10 minutes per session at the start and then, can gradually go up to 20, 30, 40 minutes, with a maximum of 60 minutes per session. The more or less significant reactions of aches and pins and needles can be felt during the first 2 or 3 weeks in the back, knee, legs, shoulders and joints of the body and then disappear after 2 or 3 weeks.

## 2. MAIN POSITIONS IN STANDING LIKE A TREE; STANDING

The positions numbered below from 1 to 5 are considered as the fundamental part of the exercise for health purposes and the ones from 6 to 8 as the fundamental part for combat. These 8 positions, depending on their intensity or practice, form the most frequently used principles in Standing Like a Tree.

The first position, having the least amount of physical intensity, is used both as preparation for starting an exercise and as a final exercise to end this type of activity and go on to the others.

The physical intensity of the 2nd position is increased because the arms are raised and the legs bent. Generally, the more the arms are raised and the legs are bent, the more intense the exercise is.

- 1st position Hands on the back

Feet shoulder width apart. Beginners can place their feet pointing outwards at the start, and then place them later. Legs should be straight with. The hands are on the back with palms turned backwards. The fingers are separated from each other. Gradually relax the shoulders.

- 2nd position Lift the hands whilst relaxing the shoulders

Feet shoulder width apart. Knees should be bent at 2-3 cm in the beginning, and then gradually increase until you begin to feel some pain. Lift the elbows to the sides, place hands above the navel with the palms facing the sky. The distance between the hands and the body should not exceed 33 cm. Gradually relax the shoulders.

- 3rd position With the chest straight, pull by pressing

Feet shoulder width apart. Hands are raised at a height between the chest and the shoulder with palms facing inwards. Fingers are separated as if holding something in the arms. Gradually relax the shoulders.

- 4th position Pushing forwards and backwards

Feet shoulder width apart. Hands are raised at a height between the eyebrows and shoulders with palms facing outwards. Fingers are separated as if gripping something while pushing forwards and backwards. Gradually relax the shoulders while moving the elbows.

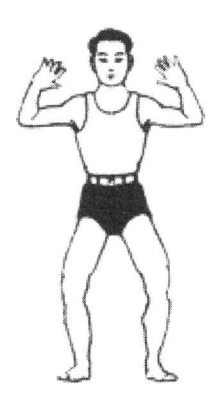

- 5th position Parting of the waters

Feet shoulder width apart. Hands are extended out to the right and left side at the height of the navel. Palms in front facing downwards. The elbows are slightly bent. Gradually relax the shoulders.

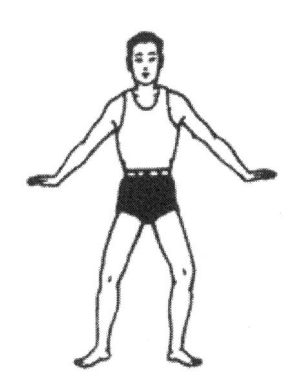

- 6th position Little step in a V shape

Feet relaxed. The forward foot is point outwards by 5-10 cm in the form of a V. Body slightly leaning in front, legs slightly bent in a seated position, leaning back. Raise the heel of the forward foot and bend the knee. The proportion of the body weight in front and at the back should be of a ratio of 40% to 60%. Hands are raised at shoulder height, elbows bent and arms rounded. Palms should face inwards or in front, with fingers separated. Relax the shoulders whilst gradually lifting the elbows. Face forwards.

- 7th position Feet apart

Feet wide apart. The heel of the forward foot should be raised and the knee pushed forward. The rear foot should be placed on the ground. Squeeze the buttocks inwards by tightening the anus. Lean backwards in a seated position. The hands, in a push-and-pull position, are raised at a height above the shoulders. The palms should face forwards. (Another similar position: The hands are placed at the height of the stomach with the palms turned downwards, as if they were holding the head of a tiger: also known as "holding the tiger").

## CHAPTER II: UPRIGHT POSITION

- 8th position Contra-step:

Feet wide apart. The heel of the forward foot is turned inwards and the knee slightly bent. The forward foot is turned outwards. The leg behind should be kept straight, without lifting the heel. The body is slightly bent forward. The proportion of the body weight in front and behind is of a ratio of a 60% to 40 in the beginning, and then moves progressively to a 70% to 30% ratio. The body and the head are turned behind, with gaze towards the heel of the foot.

If the left leg is in front, then the right hand and its palm face upwards and the left hand and its palm face downwards. The elbows are slightly bent as if to push something. The same position is reversed if the right leg is in front. The position of the elbows does not change. An easier position to maintain would be to raise the arm corresponding to the leg in front, as illustrated below.

# CHAPTER III
# HOW DOES ONE MASTER THE INTENSITY OF THE ZHAN ZHUANG MOVEMENT?

## 1. THE CHOICE BETWEEN THE PRACTICE OF THE HAND OR THE FOOT

When the body is upright, the arms are not needed for support. The hands adapt quite naturally to flexible activities. The form of their joints is both relaxed and limp. Therefore, we can consider that the arm and the hand are extremely flexible. The shape of the lower limbs is more solid and the joints are tighter and thicker. This creates a narrower joint to the torso that is better adapted to support and propel the body.

The analyzer of movement, located somewhere in the cerebral cortex, plays an important role in the body's movements. The front part of the cerebral cortex which regulates the movement of the body acts via a direct link with the muscles. In this central zone, in front of the cerebral cortex, the stimulation is greater, the distribution of work more specialised and the control stricter. The zone receives messages of stimulation from the joints, muscles and the skeleton, thereby being aware of its own stance and movement.

The size of the area occupied by the various parts of the body to the corresponding zones of the analyzer of the brain is linked, not to their physical shape, but to distribution of the functions in the body. For example, the areas corresponding to the lip, tongue and hand in the cerebral cortex are relatively large. The human hand, because of the diversity of its role, the complexity and the frequency of its activities, has a larger cortical zone than the foot. For the cortical zones of the five fingers are most important. Amongst the five fingers, the thumb and index finger have a larger cortical zone. If a drawing was made of the cerebral cortex for the different parts of the body, it would indicate the location of the muscles to which they correspond. The inside of the cerebral cortex corresponds to the hand and the face with a more sensitive zone occupied by the fingers and the mouth. The result would be an opposite image of the normal view of the body, which would show from top to bottom a small foot, a small leg, a big hand and a big face.

It has long been said that man starts to age by the legs, that age can be calculated by studying the legs. The secret of long life therefore rests in exercising the legs. In Chinese martial arts, there are also expressions such as "combat is 30% by hand and 70% by foot, "fight with a man as if to pull out weeds, act with the foot as with the hand, focusing on the root". On the other hand, concerning the role of strength, it's true that "strength is born in the foot, developed by the leg, transferred by the back and realized by the fingers". It can also be said that "when fighting someone strong, power comes from pushing down on the foot", and also that in a combat technique the foot's role is more important than that of the hand.

According to the analysis done during autopsies, the weight of the lower limbs is 3 times that of the upper limbs. For example, for a total weight of 59.70 kg, the head weighs 4.14 kg, the trunk 25.08 kg, the two lower limbs 22.86 kg and the two upper limbs 7.62 kg. Measuring the increase in heart rate also proves that significantly more effort is needed to bend the legs than to raise the hands. Moreover, the largest muscles are found in the lower limbs.

However, the corresponding zones in the area of the cerebral cortex are relatively small and the distribution of work is not as specialised as for the upper limbs, even though the area of the lower limbs is bigger and consequently stronger. This is why there is a greater capacity to transform the physiology and functional structure as well as physically improve the lower limbs of the body than the upper ones. A substantial structural and functional change in the body can be achieved by developing elasticity in the lower muscles in order to increase their flexibility, and thereby reinforcing the cerebral cortex's control via the nervous system of the lower muscles.

In conclusion, in the practice of Zhan Zhuang, training the lower muscles is more important than training the upper ones. It could be said that is it is more effective to practice from the bottom (feet and legs) upwards (hands) than the other way around. Focus on carrying out the exercise in this order: feet, legs, thighs, buttocks, kidneys, chest, back, shoulders, neck, head, elbows and lastly hands. The aim of training from bottom up is the key problem and should be taken into account.

In ancient times, it was said "The technique of the hand should be taught without teaching the technique of the foot; if not, the student will be stronger than his master", meaning that the foot's technique is more important than the hand's. At the same time, there are other contradictions such as movement and stability, posture and mind, cause and effect. These three notions contrast the brain and muscle; their mastery is achieved in the first phase of practice. In the second phase, it is necessary to know the distinction between the upper and the lower limbs, the tense and the relaxed and the core (essence) and extremity. In the third stage, it is necessary to know the distinction between the total/partial and interior/exterior Qi. The three phases and the nine pairs of contradictions mentioned above form the basis of Wu (aim) of Zhang Zhuang. It shows a big difference between the notions of movement and stability, stance and mind and cause and the result in Zhan Zhuang and other physical activities.

The aim of physical activities is to gain a healthy body, to cure diseases and to avoid getting diseases. In ancient times, the scholar, Guanzi, referred to "the art of the mind", what we now call "martial arts" or "the art of the wrist". This shows the importance of training the brain by means of muscular exercises. It corresponds to the notion of the second voluntary movement: of contraction/relaxation of the muscles while at rest.

Generally, the notion of "movement" is known as for example when a bird that flies or a horse that walks etc. These movements consist of moving of the limbs. While, movement without changing position or moving the limbs, involving a change only in posture and using the mind, is the practice known as movement in stability. 2700 years ago, the scholar Guanzi, said "hold still without moving", "Taoism is in stability" and the scholar Laozi, said "Even without motion, the body is continually moving". Nei Jing remarked in a medical publication: "Keeping the mind focused and the body motionless makes the muscles work in harmony". It can thus be seen that there is a considerable difference between these oriental and western philosophies; one based on Zhan Zhuang and the other on martial arts or actual physical activities.

| Phases | Contradictions | Solutions |
| --- | --- | --- |
| • 1st phase<br>• Brain and muscle | • Movement and stability<br>• Posture and intention<br>• Cause and effect | • Standard movement and stability<br>• Movement in stability and posture<br>• Spiritual movement |
| • 2nd phase<br>• Part and entity | • Big and small<br>• Tense and relaxed<br>• Root and extremity | • Hand and foot practice<br>• Tension and relaxation movement<br>• Movement of feet in stability |
| • 3rd phase<br>• Interior and exterior | • Qi and Wu<br>• Part and entity<br>• Interior and exterior | • Qi study<br>• Wu study<br>• Ordering of Wu<br>• Naming of Wu<br>• Second voluntary movement etc. |

Table of the 3 phases and 9 pairs of contradictions

## 2. CLASSIFICATION OF THE DIFFERENT INTENSITIES OF MOVEMENT

It is well known that excessive consumption of medication is harmful; it is the same for food. Diseases may result from eating more than the body requires. The same principle applies to physical training, including Zhan Zhuang. The intensity of movement should be progressively increased from low to high, from a simple activity to one that is more complex, until the goal is achieved by regular training Generally, taking one's level of fitness into account, the intensity of movement has to be determined in an accurate and proper manner.

There are 5 categories of intensity of movement: intensity without effect; maintained intensity; reinforced intensity; excessive intensity and insufficient intensity.

## A. INTENSITY WITHOUT EFFECT

The muscles and nerves of the body react when they are stimulated. These reactions become apparent in flexing the muscles, and when these movements reach a certain level they trigger changes in the physiological functioning: for example, changes in blood circulation, breathing etc. When muscle activity is insufficient and the duration of movement is too short to lead to a significant change, this leads to a movement of intensity without effect that can be identified by the lack of change before and during the movement.

## B. MAINTAINED INTENSITY

This becomes apparent by a sensation of well-being in the body during the practice of Zhan Zhuang with relatively stable breathing and a slight increase in pulse. This balanced intensity of movement is called maintained and is particularly suitable for beginners and old people.

Maintained intensity provides positive stimulation and encourages control in the cerebral cortex and stretching that stimulates the nervous system. This increases blood circulation and breathing which helps the body fight infection.

## C. REINFORCED INTENSITY

This movement, indicated by a slight sensation of pins and needles and aches during training, is called reinforced intensity, in which a significant change in the body results in an increase in fitness level and health. During this phase, the production of flexible movements in the muscles is continuous and the pulse and respiration are maintained at a high level

## D. EXCESSIVE INTENSITY

When the intensity of movement exceeds the body's tolerance level, it is called an excessive intensity. At this stage, certain parts of the joints and muscles of the body become extremely painful. After training, symptoms of an excessive intensity" are weakness, pain in the limbs, discomfort, sleepless nights, inattentive mind, inability to rapidly recover or even a lack of appetite.

## E. INSUFFICIENT INTENSITY

The muscles and nerves must be regularly exercised to maintain a certain level of physiological functioning. Even after a period of Zhan Zhuang training where the effects have become established, if it ceases for any reason, the lack of stimulation will lead to a steady drop back towards the previous level. The longer the period of non-practice, the greater the decline. It will be evident by the recurrence of the former sensations of pins and needles and aches again while holding the same positions.

The five intensities of movement described above are designed to be adapted to the fitness level of each person. It is up to the individual to look for and discover how to control and maintain his/her own intensity of movement during training. For example, at the beginning of the exercise, we can say that by bending 2cm the legs, it is the maintained intensity" and at 4cm it is the reinforced intensity.

After a period of training, resistance is strengthened; the former 2 cm becomes the intensity without effect, 4 cm becomes the maintained intensity, 6 cm becomes the reinforced intensity and 8 cm becomes the excessive intensity ,and so on and so forth.

## 3. MOVEMENT INTENSITY FACTORS

Participants need to master a suitable intensity according to certain criterion. This criterion regarding the intensity of movement is made up of several aspects: a subjective criterion, an objective criterion, one concerning duration and one concerning the recovery period.

### A. THE SUBJECTIVE FACTOR

This is based on the participant' own reactions, and on the aches and pins and needles in the arms and legs. However, there should not be sensations of heaviness in the chest due to excess pain, heartbeats breathlessness and other abnormal effects.

### B. THE OBJECTIVE FACTOR

This is mostly based on the increase in the number of heartbeats, grouped in the following manner:

- Weak type: an increase of 10 to 20 beats during training. This is suitable for elderly people having a fairly poor fitness level and for people suffering from heart disease and high blood pressure.
- Average type: an increase of 20 to 30 beats during training. This is suitable for elderly and weak people but more for those having general illnesses.
- Normal type: an increase of 30 to 50 beats during training, suitable for people in good health.
- Strong type: an increase of 50 to 70 beats during training, suitable for fit people.

Those practitioners who do not obtain an increase in the number of beats during training need to reinforce the intensity of movement depending on their physical capabilities, in order to reach an efficient level of training.

## C. THE DURATION FACTOR

For each training session the duration should be determined by the fitness level and the position chosen. Beginners can start with 5 minutes and gradually increase to 40 minutes, with a maximum of one hour. If the duration is too short, the result will be unsatisfactory and if it is too long, fatigue will arise. It is a good idea to regulate both the duration and position of training according to circumstances. Generally speaking, the duration is relatively reduced when one practises a strong position and vice versa. People having a poor level of fitness must be more careful, to avoid forcing or repeating the same position 2 or 3 times.

## D. THE RECOVERY PERIOD FACTOR

The recovery phase is defined as the time measured between the cessation of the training and the complete disappearance of the corresponding physical reactions. This recovery period depends on the fitness level of the individual and the length of time. The duration whether long or short, is an aid in regulating the intensity of movement. If the fatigue caused by training has not disappeared after a night of rest, the intensity is too strong and should be reduced a little. If recovery is too fast, it can be increased accordingly. This regulation makes the training more effective.

The criteria mentioned above are only principles. How are they used in practice? It is up to each person to apply them according to his own case.

## 4. CALCULATION OF THE INTENSITY OF MOVEMENT

It is far more difficult to control the intensity of movement in practice. The metric system is used in order to be able to measure it correctly. It proves that the more complicated the movement, the greater it is.

### A. CALCULATION OF HEIGHT IN CM

During training, the legs should be bent. Normally, it's not possible to measure the exact extent of bending other than by making an visual guess by experience. By correctly measuring the height of the flexion of the body by a point of reference, we can calculate precisely in cm the flexion of the legs. The bigger the measurement, the greater the intensity of movement. This is at the same time a scientific and a simple measurement.

### B. CALCULATION IN MM OF THE VERTICAL PROJECTION FROM THE BODY'S CENTRE OF GRAVITY

After practising for some time, the fitness level is improved. To go a step farther, in addition to being able to significantly lower the height of the body, it's possible to regulate the centre of gravity. This relatively small modification can only be measured in mm. Taking for example a vertical position; there is a 90 degree angle between the line linking the shoulder joints and the hip joints and the ground. If the centre of gravity of the body projects over the central part of the arch of the foot, the intensity of movement is relatively small. On the other hand, it is greater if the projection of the centre of gravity is more towards the back. The increase of intensity of muscular movement occurs to maintain the body's equilibrium which has been affected by displacing the centre of gravity.

Moving backwards is limited to the point where the tip of the foot is not raised. The more the body leans back, away from the centre, the more the movement intensifies. This method, considered as a way to increase the intensity of movement progressively, should be applied without bending the head or the back, neither pushing the hip backwards nor pushing the stomach forward by raising the head. This method should not be used by old or sick people.

### C. CALCULATION OF THE SPIRITUAL ACTIVITIES IN µM

The aim of practising Zhan Zhuang is to use the cerebral cortex and is a special training for the muscles at rest in order to create a second involuntary movement...

At this phase of advanced training, without moving the limbs, the Shen Qi (energy) changes and manifests itself in three ways: Jing (vitality), Qi (energy that circulates in the body) and Shen (spirituality).

It is difficult to measure the Shen Qi that correlates to spiritual activities; for example, focusing on the top of the head, carrying something, supporting with the shoulder, pulling with the hands, straddling something, twisting the back etc. We can see the state of Shen Qi but it is very difficult to measure it accurately, even using micrometers (µm). Although the difference in Shen Qi is very small, the corresponding increase in the intensity of movement is relatively large. Beginners have trouble mastering this method.

## 5. THE PRINCIPLE OF ADJUSTMENT AND DISTRIBUTION ON YI (PURPOSE) AND XING (POSTURE)

Xing depicts posture and Yi depicts purpose in the exercise. Xing, Yi and duration make up the three main factors of adjustment and distribution of the intensity of movement. Being able to coordinate the first two of these helps us to control the intensity of movement. There are 6 ways to achieve this, as described below.

## A. ELIMINATING YI AND SUPPRESSING XING

Eliminating Yi means removing purpose. Suppressing Xing suggests that the legs are not bent more than 10 cm. This position is relatively easy on the arms and legs and is suitable for those beginners who possess a certain level of control.

## B. ELIMINATING YI AND EXAGGERATING XING

Any position where the legs are bent more than 10 cm has a significant effect on Xing. With practice, participants can bend the legs more and raise the arms without effort.

## C. REDUCING YI AND XING AT THE SAME TIME

On one hand, for the sick, reducing Yi is useful as an imaginary controlled exercise to aid healing, while on the other hand, for healthy participants, it is useful for improving flexibility. It is suitable for beginners who have trouble concentrating.

## D. REDUCING YI AND INCREASING XING

This method involves significant bending and imaginary controlled activities or flexing internal muscles in order to increase the intensity of movement. It is suitable for experienced participants and not for beginners or the sick.

## E. EXAGGERATING YI AND SUPPRESSING XING

Exaggerating Yi means doing something very purposefully, for example, the movements of Expanding/Tightening, Sliding/Cutting, Pulling/Lifting which involve slight bending during the exercise. In addition, it's necessary to increase the focus. This method is suitable for people in good health.

### F. INCREASING YI AND XING AT THE SAME TIME

This method involves increasing the degree of flexion of the arms and legs and spiritual activities. It is suitable for strong people.

## 6. COORDINATION OR XING (POSTURE), YI (INTENTION), LI (STRENGTH), QI (ENERGY) AND SHEN (VIGOUR)

Zhan Zhuang is one of the most important physical activities to build fitness. Its main aspects are Xing (posture), Yi (intention), Li (strength), Qi (energy from breathing) and Shen (vital source).

The coordination of these 5 aspects is fundamental during the exercise, because this affects the intensity of movement and the effectiveness of the exercise. Below are some analyses of these aspects.

### A. HAVING XING WITHOUT I IS AN "EMPTY XING"

An exercise which involves bending and flexing the muscles, but which is not purposeful, that is to say without engagement of the muscles at rest, is a movement that has no effect. It is called "Empty Xing". The intensity of movement is relatively low.

### B. HAVING I WITHOUT XING DOES NOT INCREASE STRENGTH

Concentrating too much on purpose but not on the bent position of the body does not strengthen it. Its intensity of movement is weak and the exercise is ineffective.

The degree of flexion is needed to be increased if the physical condition allows.

### C. HAVING YI WITHOUT LI IS AN "EMPTY YI"

Flexing the muscles requires a certain amount of strength. Intention becomes ineffective if strength is inadequate, and the exercise is similar to a level of "Empty Yi". Consequently, the practice of Yi depends on the posture.

### D. HAVING STRENGTH WITHOUT I IS INEFFICIENT

Some people are very strong but cannot correctly practice the art of intention, and being unfamiliar with flexible movement they are not able to use their strength effectively. This, in turn, reduces the role of Yi in practice and as such, reduces the intensity of movement.

### E. HAVING STRENGTH WITHOUT QI IS A BANAL STRENGTH

During the exercise, because of the dilation of muscles, the consumption of oxygen in the body is increased. This loss has to be recovered by proper breathing, otherwise one will feel stifled by a lack of oxygen. Therefore, we can say that breathing influences the quality of movement.

### F. HAVING QI WITHOUT STRENGTH IS NOT PRACTICAL

Good breathing combined with movement, but without the use of muscular strength controlled by the Yi does not increase the ability for combat. This is not an ideal exercise.

### G. HAVING I WITHOUT SHEN IS NOT OF THE HIGHEST LEVEL

Even if participants correctly master the training of Yi and obtain Yi, Li and Qi are not yet perfected. They still need Shen, which characterizes vigor of a body by being both comfortably relaxed and extensively spiritual. The Shen can also link Yi/Li/Qi and is the highest level of the practice of Zhan Zhuang.

## H. HAVING SHEN – YI – LI – QI, ALWAYS BE PREPARED

When one gets to a superior level, it is not only necessary to master the Shen/Yi/Li/Qi but also to always be alert enough even when Shen/Li/Qi is unleashed at any moment.

# 7. RELATIONSHIP BETWEEN THE DEGREE OF FLEXION AND THE INTENSITY OF MOVEMENT

## A. RELATIONSHIP BETWEEN THE PIVOT POINT AND THE INTENSITY OF MOVEMENT

During the exercise, keep the body straight without leaning forward or backward. The line connecting the shoulder joints and the hip should form an angle of 90° with the ground. On this basis, the three pressure points of the foot are the following:

- Weight on the arch of the foot

The sole of the foot and the heel are raised off the ground in such a way that the arch of the foot supports the entire weight of the body. The exercise in this position has a rather weak intensity and is suitable for beginners.

- Weight on the sole of the foot

With the sole pushing against the ground and the heel slightly lifted, the sole supports the weight of the body and the centre of gravity is slightly forward. To avoid leaning forward, the leg muscles should be somewhat contracted to maintain balance, thereby increasing the intensity of movement.

- Weight on the heel

The heel and the sole should be flat on the floor with the body in a seated position so that the heel supports the weight of the body. The exercise necessitates gradually moving the centre of gravity behind the heel. The more this is done, the less stable the body becomes and the more the leg muscles must be contracted to maintain balance. The intensity of movement gradually increases; therefore, this is not particularly suitable for beginners.

## B. RELATIONSHIP BETWEEN THE SURFACE OF THE FOOT AND THE INTENSITY OF MOVEMENT

The surface of the foot touching the ground and the angle between the ankle and the ground play an important role in the intensity of movement in the legs.

- Flat surface

It's more convenient if you choose a flat surface or a room to carry out the exercise and if possible, it is advisable to use a mat to reduce the impact of the ground.

- Cushion under the heel

The heel can be raised either by the slope of the ground or by placing a bag of sand underneath. It is placed higher than the sole at 10-30 degrees from the ground, increasing the angle with the ankle joint. This angle has an effect on the leg and foot muscles, which are then used at a higher degree of the intensity of movement.

- Cushion under the sole of the foot

The same method as mentioned above is used, only the sole of the foot replaces the heel. The reduction in the angle with the ankle joint increases the intensity of movement.

- Cushion under the arch of the foot

This method entails using a bag of sand placed under the arch of the foot, leaving the heel and the sole touching the ground. It increases resiliency in the legs and offers certain benefits to heal flat feet.

- Heel suspended

This method uses two long bricks or the stairs, on which the soles of the feet are placed to suspend the heels. The greater the surface suspended, the more intense the movement.

This method reduces the surface of the two feet in contact with the ground. It requires greater contraction of the muscles to maintain body balance and requires training.

c. Relationship between the position of the foot and the intensity of movement

The four foot positions are as follows:

- V-shaped

Beginners can put their feet in the shape of a V. The distance between the two heels should be around 25 to 35 cm, and 40-50 cm for the tips of the feet. The feet now form an angle of 50 to 70 degrees (usually 60 degrees).

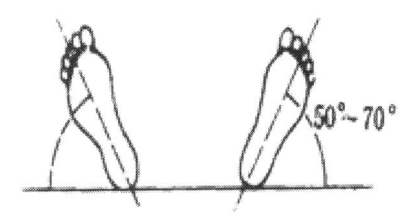

- Parallel Shape

The distance between the heels and the tips of the feet is almost equal. The feet are about 30 to 40 cm apart, at an angle of 70 to 90 degrees. If we compare this position with the preceding one, although the distance between the tips is somewhat modified, the intensity of leg strength is significantly increased.

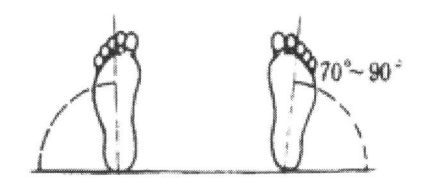

For a strictly parallel position, the distance between the soles of the feet should not be less than that of the heels, meaning that the angle is not more than 90 degrees. Otherwise, the angle should not exceed 50 degrees when placing the soles of the feet outwards. Using a position in which the soles of the feet are closer than the heels, we obtain the shape of an inverted V. This position is not only uncomfortable but more serious; it forces the knee joints inwards forming an X, without being able to apply strength outwards. This makes it difficult to release the strength created by pressing the heels against the ground.

- Bent shape

The position of the feet for the Bent shape is similar to the one for Rest. The angle between the feet is at 50 to 70 degrees and is similar to the 6th position, Small step, where the distance between the heels is 50 to 90 cm. The greater the distance (as in the Big step position), the greater the intensity of movement. This method places more weight on the back leg.

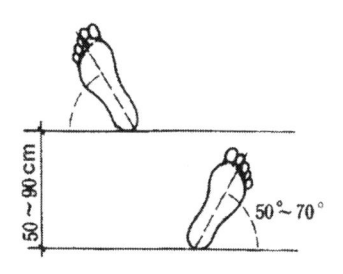

- Contra-foot shape

The method of this shape has a more significant effect than the others on the movement of the leg and back muscles. As in the Contra-foot position, the heel of the front foot is placed inward and the sole of the corresponding foot is placed outwards, forming an angle of about 0 to 50 degrees. The smaller the angle, the greater the intensity of movement. The distance between the two feet is about 60-90 cm, and the greater the distance the stronger the intensity. The body is bent forward with the weight supported primarily by the front leg, which increases the strength used during training.

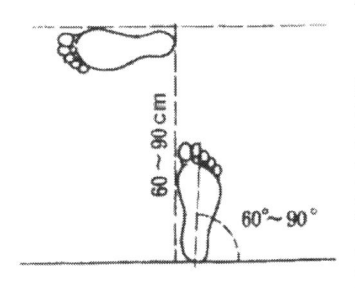

## D. RELATIONSHIP BETWEEN THE POSITION OF THE KNEE JOINT AND THE INTENSITY OF MOVEMENT

In a normal standing position, an angle of 90 degrees formed from the ground, with an angle of 180 degrees connecting from the top of the knee joint, up to the hip and shoulder joints, to the outside of the ear and down to the ankle joint.

At this angle, the body is held upright by its skeletal frame without having to contract the muscles too much to continue standing. If this position is held for a long time, the rhythm of heartbeats scarcely changes. In the exercise of Zhan Zhuang, the top of the body must remain fixed while adjusting the angle of the knee joints to 170, 160, 150 degrees and so on to a minimum of 90 degrees.

At this time, the more the body is lowered, the smaller the angle of the knees becomes. This also increases the intensity of movement and the heartbeat.

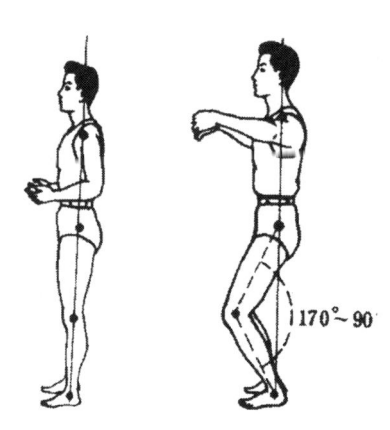

## E. RELATIONSHIP BETWEEN THE POSITION OF THE HIP JOINT AND THE INTENSITY OF MOVEMENT

During training, if the angle between the line connecting the centre of the shoulder and hip joints to the ground is at 90 degrees, then the smaller the hip joint angle is at, the higher the intensity of movement is. This angle, however, should never exceed 90 degrees, as indicated in (1) and (2). Obviously, it is very difficult to get to this position (2), which serves only as an aim. It also demonstrates how to gradually increase the intensity of the exercise by changing positions. Before being called "Standing Like a Tree", the practice was called "The Three Parallel Lines", which is to say, the vertical shoulder joint line is parallel to the hip, knee and ankle joint lines and the horizontal hip joint line is parallel to the knee joint line. In reality, the most common position is shown in (3), with the back bent and the body leaning forward. Although the angle of the hip joint is reduced, the shoulder joint angle is also reduced in relation to the ground. Since the corresponding centre of gravity does not cross the zone supported by the feet, the intensity of movement is relatively low.

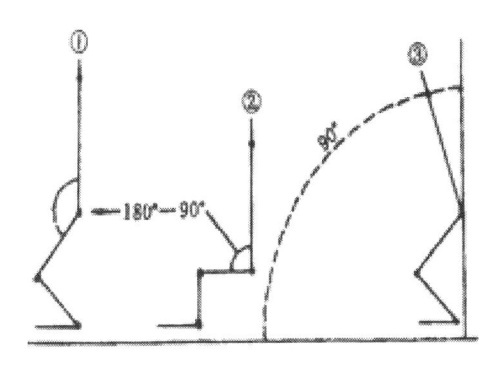

## F. RELATIONSHIP BETWEEN THE POSITION OF THE ANKLE JOINT AND THE INTENSITY OF MOVEMENT

Even if the upper body is kept in a fixed position and the legs are considerably bent, the intensity of movement is not increased if the knee goes over the tip of the foot. The angles between the knee and ankle joints and the ankle and tip of the foot are relatively small and should not be less than 45 degrees. On the other hand, the bigger the angle is with the knee (which should not pass the tip of the foot), and the more the centre of gravity of the surface supporting the body weight is backward, the greater the intensity of movement is. This angle should not exceed 90 degrees.

## G. RELATIONSHIP BETWEEN THE POSITION OF THE SHOULDER JOINT AND THE INTENSITY OF MOVEMENT

The height at which the arms are give a varying result in this particular exercise. If we take the shoulder joint as the central axis, the smaller the angle between the elbow and the surface of the ribs below the armpits, the closer the elbow is to the body, the lower is the intensity of movement. For example, the angle of the elbows in the 2nd position, "Lifting the arms and relaxing the shoulders", is about 45 degrees. On the contrary, the bigger the angle is, the higher the intensity, as long as the angle does not exceed 90 degrees, as shown in position number 4, "Push and lift".

## H. RELATIONSHIP BETWEEN THE POSITION OF THE ELBOW JOINT AND THE INTENSITY OF MOVEMENT

Spreading the arms gives a lower intensity, with a minimum of 45 degrees, as presented in position number 2, "Lifting the arms while relaxing the shoulders". However, the more the arms are stretched forward and the bigger the elbow joint angle becomes, the higher the intensity of movement is, as indicated in position number 5, "Parting of the waters".

## I. RELATIONSHIP BETWEEN THE POSITION OF THE WRIST AND THE INTENSITY OF MOVEMENT

Even though its muscles and bones may be small, the hand is very flexible and sensitive and its movements are agile and intuitive. This is due to a large reflex zone in the brain that controls the nervous system corresponding to the hand, and which has numerous possibilities of action.

The intensity of movement intensity is relatively small when the wrist joint is facing downwards in a limp state. It is increased by extending the wrist while holding the fingers straight, and even more by the wrists "gripping something" while spreading the fingers apart.

# CHAPTER IV
# THE WORK OF INTENTION IN ZHAN ZHUANG

The work of intention (I) in the practice of Zhan Zhuang can be defined as mind training via an intellectual exercise of thought, analysis, synopsis, judgement, reason and education.

There are two types of work of intention (AS). One is controlled AS and the other is the animated AS. The two types of AS create different effects; the first one's suitable for beginners and the second one's for more advanced practitioners.

## 1. THE ACTION OF RELAXATION

An action of relaxation involves focusing the mind on one part of the body by concentrating on the nerve in order to control the muscles. Each time this is done, one must think about the initial state of the muscles and follow their evolution closely. The aim is to assure that this state corresponds to a phase of relaxation in the mind, on one hand in order to develop the ability to relax the muscles, and on the other hand, the awareness of this relaxation. When the muscles are too stimulated by elastic movement, people lacking the relaxation training are not aware of this overload and the muscles therefore stay contracted. Consequently, fatigue quickly sets in. In mastering the technique of relaxation, premature fatigue is avoided because the muscles contract under pressure and less energy is used if they are relaxed. This principle thus has to be applied in the Zhan Zhuang exercise, and to achieve it, several methods of practice will be outlined below.

## A. RELAXATION OF THE MIND

Relaxing the mind is a warm-up before training. It is necessary to get rid of all bad thoughts before starting the practice.

Relaxation of the mind plays an important role in the practice of Zhan Zhuang. It develops conviction. However, it is not always easy to have a calm mind at the beginning of an exercise, especially for beginners and the weak, who, for whatever reason, through lack of conviction or reactions from training, get bored quickly even after a minute of training. This can be interpreted as an inability to relax the mind and stay calm. However, after a period of 3 to 4 weeks of practice, one is able to get past the reaction of aches and pins and needles and enter into the phase of relaxation and well-being. At this point, we control ourselves more easily and can practise about 40 to 60 minutes without any difficulty. When one is able to focus on the mind without thinking of anything at all, we can say that the mind is relaxed.

## B. RELAXATION OF EXPRESSION

Another way to focus the mind during training is to relax, by reminding oneself about happy things or interesting stories in order to keep the mind entertained. At this stage, the expression of "almost laughing without smiling" appears on the face.

This method of expression in relaxation has a solid scientific basis, because when the brain is aroused by pleasant things, the muscles of the face relax into a smile, for example, when we burst out laughing watching a comedy or listening to funny stories. It provides a way to relax the mind and muscles that leads to a feeling of well-being.

## C. RELAXATION BY BREATHING

Ideally, one should try to permanently control the shoulder muscles, which are easily contracted, so that the muscles don't get tense, the shoulder is not raised, the respiration remains smooth and natural and that there's no breathlessness in the chest. In case, the phenomena described above appear, first take a deep breath to open up the rib cage as much as possible, and then stretch the spine upwards and at the same time lean on either side. Finally, breathe out as much as possible to revert the rib cage to its initial position and de-contract the muscles. This should be done once every 4 to 5 minutes, each time taking 2 or 3 deep breaths.

### D. RELAXATION BY SMALL MOVEMENT

Relaxation by small movement is designed to relax the muscles by little shifts in the body's joints. It involves moving the joints in every direction every 5 to 10 minutes while maintaining the same stance. The aim is to always be able to control the posture, which should be perfect, and assure that the muscles are relaxed.

### E. RELAXATION BY ACTIVELY CHANGING POSITION

After 10 to 20 minutes of training, when the sensations of aches and pins and needles in certain parts of the active muscles are too unbearable to endure, the arms can be lowered, the legs straightened and the hands gently squeezed or shaken a few times to loosen the joints a little. The exercise can then be continued after changing position. Modification depends on the individual's reaction, the aim being to relax the muscles by moving slightly.

### F. RELAXATION BY PASSIVELY CHANGING POSITION

Modifications in position should be carried out according to the instructions of the trainer or guide who controls the participants' movements. They observe and then will ask for certain incorrect movements to be changed. This can be by touching, shaking, vibrating, holding, rocking, pulling and even offering suggestions to help the participants relax their muscles.

## 2. THE ACTION OF IMAGINATION

Also called the action of supposition or the action of recall, this effective method involves guiding the brain's layers to reach a state of control. Its aim is to develop the capacity for calmness and concentration and to remove unnecessary thoughts by the following methods:

### A. LOOKING INTO THE DISTANCE

By staring into the distance during training, the mind is focused because of the reaction of the optical nerve is on a fixed object. This can be practised inside as well as outside, as long as the object is appealing.

### B. LISTENING FROM A DISTANCE

This method involves listening from a distance to help build concentration. Elders used to say: "Focus within while listening to the raindrops falling from the skies." Nowadays, we can listen to radio, music programmes, literature, theatre and news while practising Zhan Zhuang. This is an effective way to concentrate and banish feelings of boredom ensuing from long periods of exercise.

### C. HOLDING AN OBJECT

Weak participants can use certain objects (for example, a bar) and hold them to reduce fatigue by relaxing the muscles. However, those who are strong can simply imagine holding objects in the arms.

Another example is to imagine moving through water with the arms pointing upwards, as if less strength was required. After practising for a while, one may experience the feeling of lightness, called "the sensation of forgetting the limbs".

### D. WALKING ON COTTON

Walking on cotton is a method designed to help relax the lower body muscles. It involves imagining that one is on a thick, soft cotton cushion and every 3 to 5 minutes, lean slightly to the right and left or occasionally grip the ground gently with the toes.

Due to changing the centre of gravity, one can feel the different sensations in the lower limb muscles caused by their contraction/relaxation, as well as their influence on the stomach muscles.

### E. HOLDING A BALLOON IN THE ARMS

Holding a balloon in the arms is a method of training the nerves at the end of the fingers in order to increase their reactivity and sensitivity. Start by imagining holding a light balloon with enough strength to stop it escape but without squeezing it so much that it bursts. Then, imagine holding a large balloon (or a watermelon) that becomes heavier and heavier, in order to increase the intensity of movement.

### F. MOVING FORWARD IN WATER

Moving forward in water develops a rapid and sensitive reaction at the end of the nerve in the lower body. To do this we can imagine ourselves standing in lukewarm water that is slowly flowing onto the instep of the foot. Then, we start to walk feeling a sensation of resistance to the water (its height would depend on the participant's physical fitness and can go up to the chest). Then, the same situation can be imagined, but this time in mud to increase the intensity of movement. It is obvious that mud will have more resistance than water.

## 3. FLEXIBLE MUSCLE MOVEMENT

### A. INTRODUCTION

People who practise conventional sports without doing special training can put their working muscles into movement by shifting. This type of movement is called voluntary movement. However, it cannot initiate movement in the working muscles and resting muscles at the same time. This type of movement is called secondary voluntary movement. Flexible movement is formed by two opposed actions; one relaxes the muscle and the other contracts/squeezes the muscles. It is carried out by mental activities that give orders to instruct the body's resting muscles to work.

This practice is the only method to exercise the secondary voluntary movement and consists in creating a new way to train the brain's nervous system. The training requires vigorous and concentrated preparation so that the brain's nervous system can remain alert.

Flexible movement, also called flexible gestures, is a mental activity to be practised by beginners of Standing Like a Tree. The training consists of developing the ability to analyze via the flexible movements of each body muscle. It is a characteristic that is special to the art of Da Cheng Quan.

Other similar activities of pulling and pushing that are also part of the flexible movement are characterized by a movement that brings together the flexible gestures of the parts of the body's muscles. This is more difficult to practise than the other exercise which stimulate, in an independent manner, a particular muscle by concentrating only on that muscle. This happens because its active zone is more limited and its movement smaller. These movements are called medium and high-level flexible movements.

### B. FLEXIBLE LEG MOVEMENT

Flexible movement of the legs is a fundamental exercise with the aim of reinforcing mobility, skill and leg and foot strength. It is also the basis of training for the 2nd voluntary movement. The different standing practice positions of Standing Like a Tree all go hand in hand with the flexible leg movement. Let us take the example of the 3rd position, "Chest straight pulling while pushing". During the exercise, while establishing the required position, remember to suddenly squeeze/contract the leg muscles and then relax them. Then, restart the process of the flexible movement after a short break.

Beginners start to feel their muscles getting limp and cannot control them after 10 to 20 rounds of training. This would need to be rigorously continued everyday to gradually be able to increase the number of rounds to 50 to 60 per session. Well-trained people can easily do 100 to 200 or 400 to 500, till 1000 rounds per session without being tired later on.

The training process for the flexible movement is as follows:

- One leg only

Choose the left or right leg for training. Do the exercise by, for example, starting with the left leg 10 to 20 times. During this time the right leg is at rest. Then, change legs. Continue in this manner, alternating the right and left leg, until you begin to feel tired.

- Both legs

Do the exercise with both the legs at the same time. At the beginning, it is a bit difficult to be able to perfectly synchronize the right and left movements. After a few sessions of training, the ability to analyze is increased.

- Alternative

The alternative exercise of the left leg and the right leg reinforces the rapidity of communication between the brain and the nervous system of the legs' muscles. Through this exercise the capacity of analysis is increased.

Example 1. Squeeze and release the muscle in the right leg and then rest. Start the same process with the left leg. Continue in this manner.

Example 2. Squeeze/release the muscle in the right leg once and then rest. Squeeze and release the muscle in the left leg twice and then rest. Start the same process changing legs and the number of flexible movements. This exercise trains the ability to control. It increases the quality of the movement by avoiding making mistakes and reinforcing the intensity of strength in each cycle of movement.

| Left  | 1 | 2 | 1 | 2 | 3 | 2 | 3 | ... |
|-------|---|---|---|---|---|---|---|-----|
| Right | 1 | 1 | 2 | 2 | 2 | 3 | 3 | ... |

Number of "contract and relax" movements in the left and right leg muscles

- The rhythm of contracting and relaxing

The rhythm of the flexible movement is linked to the problem of the length of time for which the brain can maintain one part of the muscles in a relaxed or a contracted state. It is more difficult to continue for a long period of time because it requires certain capacities of resistance. As a result, beginners can feel out of breath. This exercise, when practised for a long period of time, is unsuitable for the elderly or the sick.

- Fast rhythm: 50 to 60 times of the flexible movement per minute.
- Slow rhythm: 20 to 30 times of the flexible movement per minute.
- Prolonged rhythm: 3 to 6 times of the flexible movement per minute to start. Then, the number per minute is

gradually reduced.

## 4. ACTION OF CONNECTING

The action of connecting is a mental training exercise that is based on the solid learning of methods with respect to the actions of certain muscles. A joint is found at the centre of these muscles and one would need to develop his/her capability to connect these two muscles at rest to make them move together in the flexible movement. As such, the movement is made up of several units or pieces of muscles at rest.

The action is usually started by connecting two points, for example, the leg and thigh, and then increasing to three points by adding the hip, for instance, and continuing in this manner. At each increase of the connecting points, at each line created and at each increase in distance, new models of movement as well as different sensations that lead to a structural change in the body are generated.

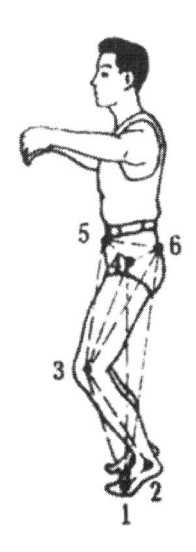

Triangular zone in action

Below are some detailed methods:

### A. TIP OF THE FOOT-HEEL-KNEE

The first line extends from the tip of the foot to the heel, passing through the centre of the ankle. A second line extends from the heel to the knee and a third, from the knee to the tip of the foot. In this way, a triangular zone is created from the sole of the foot connecting the muscles at rest in the leg, in such a way that we carry out the flexible movement (1,2,3).

### B. TIP OF THE FOOT-KNEE-HIP

The first side of the triangle is made by a line going from the tip of the foot to the centre of the knee. The second side goes from the knee to the hip and the third, from the hip to the sole of the foot. This triangular zone is used to connect the muscles at rest in the legs and thighs and to carry out the flexible movement (1,2,3).

### C. KNEE-STOMACH-HIP; TIP OF FOOT-HEEL-KNEE-STOMACH-HIP-BUTTOCKS

These zones are more complex: a triangle from the tip of the foot/hip connected to the knee/stomach can be formed. A hexagon from the tip of the foot/heel/knee/stomach/hip. Buttocks can also be formed. In this way, we connect the muscles at rest in the buttocks, stomach, hip and thigh. Secondly, the leg muscle is added and the flexible movement is created (3,4,5,6, and 1, 2, 3, 4, 5, 6).

### D. ELBOW-SHOULDER-HAND

The three peaks of the triangle are the centre of the elbow, shoulder and hand.
A triangular is formed in which the resting muscles in front and

behind the arm are connected to carry out flexible movement.

### E. THUMB-LITTLE FINGER-WRIST

This triangle is made up of the thumb, little finger and wrist. The thumb should be connected to the little finger by passing through the centre of the palm. They are then stretched outwards and the tips of the corresponding fingers are made to grasp something. The tips of the other three fingers are raised and stretched forward, the palm is pulled in, the wrist is facing downwards and the shoulder muscles are relaxed at the same time.

## 5. THE ACTION OF PULLING THE TENDON

The action of pulling the tendon is a standard exercise in the flexible movement. It is done by connecting two or several body parts or resting muscles to the joints as if they were being suddenly pulled to create a "spring" effect on both the sides or on one side with the other remaining still in order to train them to become flexible,.

The muscles at rest in the body are dealt with together and the hip, knee, shoulder and elbow joints remain fixed even while practising the flexible movement in four directions. This was formerly referred to as the "Unification of muscles".

It must be noted that this complex action also includes basic actions from the flexible muscle movement and the action of connecting, but should not be considered as a simple action. Below, some practical methods are described.

### A. BOTH FEET / BACK

Both the feet and the back form a triangular zone where the resting muscles are connected. The rapid flexible movement is applied as if to pull a spring.

## B. BOTH FEET / NECK

Both the feet and the neck form a triangular zone. In this zone, the muscles at rest in the feet, legs, thighs, hips, back, stomach and neck are connected. The rapid flexible movement is applied as if to pull a spring.

## C. BOTH HANDS / NECK

In a T-shaped posture, both the hands with the neck form a triangular zone where the resting muscles in the hands, arms, neck, shoulders and back are connected. The brisk flexible movement is then applied as if to pull a spring

## D. BOTH FEET / BACK; BOTH HANDS / BACK

In a T-shaped posture, both the feet, together with the back, form a triangular zone and both the hands, together with the neck, form another. A third triangle is formed from the hand to the neck and from the neck to the other hand with the back acting as the centre. The three triangles are then connected. The brisk flexible movement is applied in all directions.

# CHAPTER V
# THE THEORY OF ZHAN ZHUANG

## 1. THE RELATION BETWEEN MEDICINE AND PHYSICAL ACTIVITIES

Human health improves depending on its physical activity. It is the best remedy against diseases and thus, plays an important role in developing good health. Unfortunately, with life being more and more modernized, there is a lack of exercise. This reduces the heart's, stomach's and immune system's ability to function efficiently; lowers metabolism and causes blood vessels to become tenser and thus, the capacity to resist illnesses is reduced.

Not only does physical exercise contributes in improving health but it can also cure certain illnesses and prolong life by mastering certain methods.

Most physical activities produce more or less different results depending on their characteristics. The aim of studying these diverse influences is to help people choose proper ways to improve their health.

Sport Medicine is considered as a new domain in science and medicine. Research is done by studying the roles of physical activity in medicine.

The role of doctors is to cure and prevent diseases. They also have the responsibility of studying different ways that allow the improvement in health and propose offering effective methods to cure and control diseases.

It goes without saying that for certain patients, physical activity cannot be used as therapy. In this case, in order to have a good balance of exercise and rest, the following facts must be taken into consideration:

- Control of the intensity of movement intensity;
- Improvement in the method practised e.g. breathing;
- Rest after training.

Young people have no problems with these aspects. However, elderly people must be careful in measuring properly the extent and accuracy of their practice.

## 2. DIAGRAM EXPLAINING HOW ZHAN ZHUANG WORKS AND ITS EVOLUTION OF WORK

After a certain period of practice in a fixed position the brain becomes agitated. One would then need to work on the ideas and sensations that arise. This process is relatively difficult to establish spontaneously and to maintain especially at the beginning of an exercise. This phase can be called "The period of selfish ideas". In order to resist, one can think of good times, breathe slowly and imagine flexible movements such as walking etc.

Gradually, these reactions are acquired in the body: sensations of aches; pins and needles or; pain. This phenomenon is called "new and strange excitement" or "message" or "the Qi sensation". It acts on what is called the sensory system of the body. These sensors incite electric impulses in the nervous system that are transferred to the brain. After having analyzed the messages, it sends tests to the changes in sensations of aches and pins and needles. This reflex is called the "reflex of study and control". By maintaining the Zhan Zhuang position, it travels via a transitional nerve and gets to its main target, the muscle.

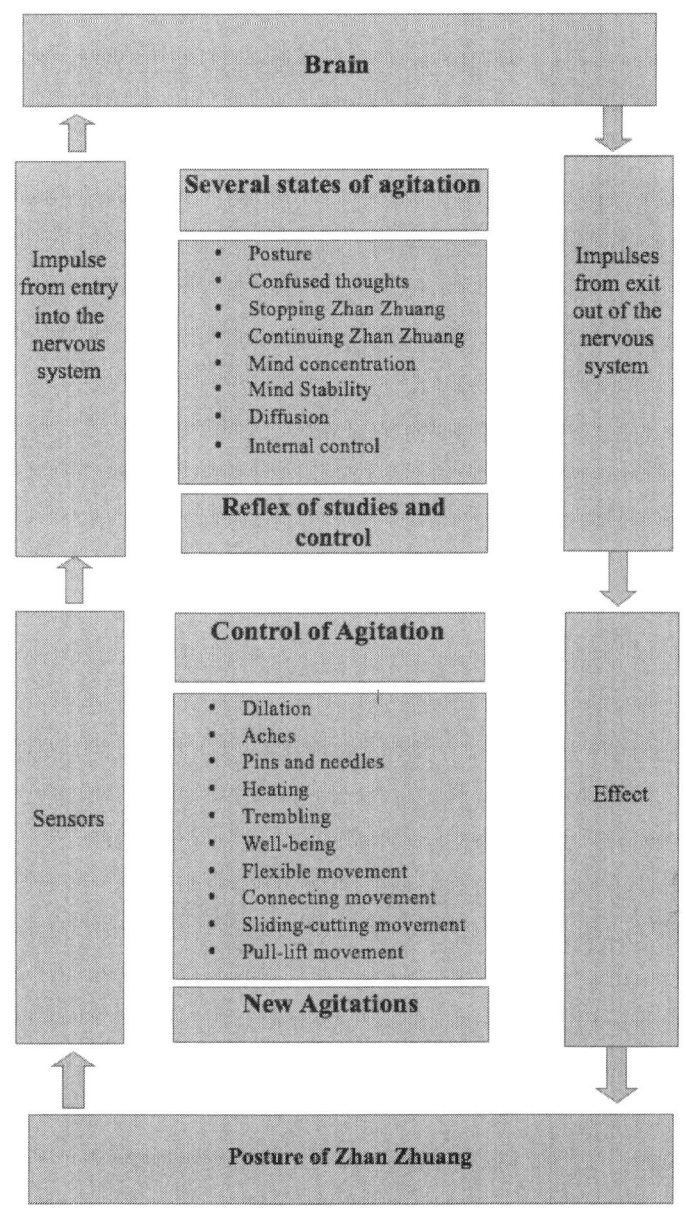

```
                    ┌─────────────────────────┐
                    │          Brain          │
                    └─────────────────────────┘
                         ↑               ↓
┌──────────┐      ┌─────────────────────────┐      ┌──────────┐
│          │      │ Several states of agitation│    │          │
│ Impulse  │      ├─────────────────────────┤      │ Impulses │
│from entry│      │  • Posture              │      │from exit │
│ into the │      │  • Confused thoughts    │      │out of the│
│ nervous  │      │  • Stopping Zhan Zhuang │      │ nervous  │
│ system   │      │  • Continuing Zhan Zhuang│     │ system   │
│          │      │  • Mind concentration   │      │          │
│          │      │  • Mind Stability       │      │          │
│          │      │  • Diffusion            │      │          │
│          │      │  • Internal control     │      │          │
│          │      ├─────────────────────────┤      │          │
│          │      │  Reflex of studies and  │      │          │
│          │      │         control         │      │          │
│          │      └─────────────────────────┘      │          │
│          │                 ↓                     │          │
│          │      ┌─────────────────────────┐      │          │
│          │      │   Control of Agitation  │      │          │
│          │      ├─────────────────────────┤      │          │
│          │      │  • Dilation             │      │          │
│          │      │  • Aches                │      │          │
│          │      │  • Pins and needles     │      │          │
│          │      │  • Heating              │      │          │
│ Sensors  │      │  • Trembling            │      │  Effect  │
│          │      │  • Well-being           │      │          │
│          │      │  • Flexible movement    │      │          │
│          │      │  • Connecting movement  │      │          │
│          │      │  • Sliding-cutting movement│   │          │
│          │      │  • Pull-lift movement   │      │          │
│          │      ├─────────────────────────┤      │          │
│          │      │     New Agitations      │      │          │
└──────────┘      └─────────────────────────┘      └──────────┘
      ↑                                                  ↓
      └──────────────────────────────────────────────────┘
                    ┌─────────────────────────┐
                    │  Posture of Zhan Zhuang │
                    └─────────────────────────┘
```

Diagram of how Zhan Zhuang works and its evolution

Resistance against aches and pins and needles is reinforced after a period of training.

These effects can also be reduced by imagining different and positive things or changing positions or angles. All of this aims mainly to reinforce reflex capability in order to have better control and then to destroy the negative phenomena.

In the mind, we must also resist the sensations of aches and pins and needles and continue practising without stopping.

After 1 or 2 weeks, the sensation of aches and pins and needles turns into trembling of the muscles accompanied by heating and perspiration of the body. Then, there is a feeling of well-being. This constitutes a turning point in practice.

The feeling of well-being should be considered as a positive agitation. The stronger it gets, the more the concentration of the brain is consolidated, reinforced and lengthened. After this comes the stage of "Internal Control".

"Internal Control" in an awakened state, is limited to a part of zones in the brain. Its role is to protect the body and stop illnesses.

It must be noted that the process mentioned above must be applied with a constant increase of rhythm in breathing and heartbeat until it is got to a stable and uniform level.

To sum up the points that were developed above, the following table that summarizes the diagram of how Zhan Zhuang works was created.

## 3. DISCUSSION ON THE DEFINITION OF STABILITY AND MOVEMENT IN STABILITY

Since ancient times, the discussion of stability and movement dates back to ancient times and has been an essential topic, closely linked to a research of the secret of good health.

Martial arts students are very familiar with the principle of "movement in stability and vice versa". In Zhan Zhuang, "movement" is defined as a shift and "stability", as a fixed position.

## A. DEFINITION OF MOVEMENT AND STABILITY

Movement and stability are relatives in the world.

- Movement and stability of shape

The body moves in space with a change in the shape of the body. For example, walking, jumping, running, turning, climbing etc. This is called "conscious movement", controlled by the brain.

- Movement and stability in physiology

Blood circulation, digestion, metabolism and basic conditions of life are "conscious movements" controlled by the body's nervous system.

- Movement and stability of the brain

It is said that the brain is in movement when it is agitated, and in stability when it is controlled. These two steps in the brain are linked to each other and are form all the processes of mental activity in the brain.
The both processes of control and agitation must be present as they function in balance. When the body is exercising, each gesture of listening, looking etc. must be directed by the brain. I call it "brain movement".
In the opposite case, if the body is still exercising without the brain's participation, I call it "brain stability".

- Methods of combination of movement and stability

Two methods to link movement and stability are: alternative and simultaneous.
For the first method, two types of movements are distinguished: non-stable and stable. In the first, the body is in movement whilst

in the second, it is in a fixed position. These two movements are practised alternately.

The second method consists in practising the two types of movement simultaneously, that is to say, keeping the same fixed (stable) position, the internal movement is carried out in the body e.g. heartbeat, breathing, agitation of the brain etc.

## B. CLASSIFICATION OF MOVEMENT

There are two main types of movement. One is a stable movement and the other a non-stable (Table B).

The movement of shifting is done by changing the shape of the body, by changing the position or by using the four limbs of the body. A greta concentration is necessary during the practice, by carefully observing things around the body. Thinking too much before moving agitates the brain. The extent of agitation depends on the intensity of movement and environment. This type of movement is similar to that of animals and is thus, called "movement like animals".

There are two types of "movement like animals". One is called "movement without effect". With this movement muscles are kept tense in a normal state. Heartbeat increases when the muscles are in brisk flexible movement. The minimum intensity of flexible movement leading to a change in heartbeat is called "Movement of threshold". Its value changes depending on the physical fitness of each person.

Movement without effect is defined as being beneath the threshold. The intensity of movement is not sufficient despite the movements of the body in attempt to significantly change the functions of the body, for example, in the case where the hands are slowly raised or during a slow walk.

Therefore, the relative definition of movement and stability at the time of movement is based on the changes of functioning in the body, instead of the movement. That is to say, changes in the heart rate, breathing as well as in the state of agitation, and control of the brain. A partial movement of body parts does not necessarily influence the entire body.

The second type of "movement like animals" is called "Movement while being unstable". An abnormal phenomenon appears while the heart rates increases due to the lack of oxygen. This is not ideal for good health. The consequence that results from this phenomenon is called "Movement while being unstable". This means that the body is in movement but with a difficulty in breathing or even stifling.

- Movement from static shifting

Movement from static shifting is the opposite to movement while shifting. The shape of the body remains stable, in a fixed position. As in the second case, participants do not need to concentrate on movement nor on things around them. It reduces the work of the brain, making it experience less agitation, which helps to get it into a controlled state. Since the movement does not cause any shifting and breathing is not difficult, the global body movement is uniform. This is called "moving like vegetables". There are two types of "movement like vegetables".

One is called "Stable and static". This means that the intensity of the functioning of the body (heartbeats, breathing etc.) is less significant or almost identical after exercising, than before. It requires relaxation of the body in order to reduce the flexible movement as much as possible. As the intensity of movement is relatively small, the change in the functioning of the body is not significant. It is especially suitable for weak people.

The second type of "movement like vegetables" is called "movement and stable". Here, movement is in stability and vice versa. Heart beat is increased, breathing is good and the brain is controlled. These three criteria must be linked. The word "movement" means actions of the body (flexible muscle movement) and stable corresponds to the brain at rest with good breathing.

It is very important to highlight that these two well-balanced activities must be carried out at the same time. To get to this, one must remove or reduce environmental influences. That is to say, the organs avoid receiving external messages. For example, the eyes are not attracted by changes that appear in its line of vision.

## 4. APPLICATION OF FLEXIBLE MOVEMENT TO "CONTRACTION AND RELAXATION" EXERCISES OF THE BOTTOM OF THE FOOT

As previously stated, the exercise of Standing Like a Tree consists in keeping the body in a fixed posture. However, the angular positions between the joints of the body's limbs are changed. For example, the knees at 180 degrees when standing and at 170-150 degrees when bent during the exercise.

Hence, the working muscles have to carry out a contracted movement in order to maintain the initial posture. Other than this movement that I call Passive Movement, there is another Active Movement that I will discuss below to complete what I described in previous chapters:

### A. PASSIVE MOVEMENT

During the exercise, the movement to contract the muscles is applied to maintain the posture. After 10 to 20 minutes, one may notice, by touching or looking, a slight wave of agitation of high frequency and speed in the leg muscles which is at the same time accompanied by "Ke Ke". The increase in temperature in the hip zone may also be at 4 to 5 degrees. An acceleration of heartbeats is also produced. Thus, a rise in temperature is produced and this results in perspiration and a feeling of well-being.

his is a passive movement and an ability that everyone has. This type of movement is caused by the change in angles linked to different joints in the body which then leads to a change in terms of weight. It thus makes the muscles produce passive actions of "contraction and relaxation". I call it PrimaryVoluntary Movement.

## B. ACTIVE MOVEMENT

The active movement is an original method from Yi Quan (or Da Cheng Quan) to teach the resting muscles the Secondary Voluntary Movement.

During this exercise, aside from the passive movement that is mandatory to maintain the body's position, another part of the muscles is at rest. They can be called the resting muscles. If they can be made to work in "contracting and relaxing" by mental movements i.e. by instruction of the brain in order to greatly increase the acceleration of heartbeats, one can say that he has mastered this active and free movement. This movement of "Contraction and Relaxation" using the muscles at rest is called Secondary Voluntary Movement for this reason.

| Classification of movement | Movement of shifting | | Movement of static shifting | |
|---|---|---|---|---|
| Nature | • Without effect<br>• Below threshold | • M. and non-S.<br>• Above threshold | • S. and non-M.<br>• Pure S. | • M. and S.<br>• M.S. unified |
| Link | E.M., S.I. | E.M., S.I. | S.O., S.I. | S.O., I.M. |
| Heartbeat | Normal | More | Reduced | More |
| Breathing | Normal | Difficult | Reduced | Reinforced |
| Brain | Agitated | Agitated | Controlled | Controlled ↔ Agitated |

Table of classification of movement

Notes:
    M. = movement; S. = stable
    E.M. = exterior movement
    IM. = interior movement
    S.O. = stable on the outside
    S.I. = stable in the inside

## C. ROLE OF THE SOLE OF THE FOOT

The most difficult action to carry out in the active movement method is moving the foot. The foot's skin with its specially developed subcutaneous tissue is hard, thick and tight. The tissue is strongly connected to the tendon's membrane. The human foot is characterized by its triangular and flexible support shape. Thanks to this, we are able to stand in a balanced position even though the surface may be uneven.

Its arched shape helps to reduce the possibility of becoming off-balanced and protects the organs, especially the brain, in the case of constant vibration experienced by the head. It also helps to reduce pressure in the nerves and blood vessels. Its flexibility also helps with walking, running and jumping. These short and long muscular tendons provide the constant strength necessary but, though very strong, they are not actively capable enough for flexible movement. This is explained by the control zone in the brain being relatively smaller for the lower body than for the upper body and the fact that less complicated tasks are done by the lower body.

They have a relatively small volume but play an important role in supporting body weight and balancing the body while standing. Their active zone is small in contrast to their vast ability to make the body and the universe shake. The foot's "Contraction/Relaxation" method is thus, specifically designed to train muscles in active movement.

| State of movement | During movement | | After movement | |
|---|---|---|---|---|
| Type of movement | M.S. | M.S.S. | M.S. | M.S.S. |
| Shoulder muscles | Tense | relaxed | quickly relaxed | relaxed |
| Sound | Firm | open and relaxed | quickly opened | open and relaxed |

| Pressure in the chest | Increases quickly | normal | quickly reduced | normal |
|---|---|---|---|---|
| Pressure in the stomach | Increases quickly | normal | quickly reduced | normal |
| Exterior resistance | Increases quickly | increase and decrease | quickly reduced | normal |
| Small blood vessel | Contracted | pressure and extension | quickly opened | normal |
| Breathing | - | natural | quick | natural |
| Pulse | + | + | more and less faster | reduced |
| Circulation in the body | Blocked | accelerated | insufficient | normal |
| Circulation in the lung | Insufficient | accelerated | full | normal |
| Heart | Insufficient | normal | quicker | normal |
| Link to renewal | Insufficient | good | quick | normal |
| Appearance | Red | normal | white | normal |

Table of functioning of the body in Movement by Shifting (M.S.) and Movement by Static Shifting (M.S.S.)

## D. ACTION OF THE SOLE OF THE FOOT IN STATIC POSITION

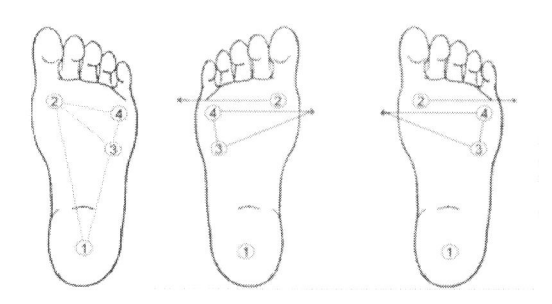

It is easy to see the difference between "movement" in running, jumping, pushing, friction etc. when the body is in a static state and movement in its true sense of the body and its limbs shifting.

Everyone knows how to do the second sense of movement. The first, which is more difficult to master, requires strong concentration with each round of "Contraction/Relaxation" needing to be thought out and directed by the brain in order to create movement in nerve endings and foot muscles.

This movement of "Contraction/Relaxation" is characterized by the mind in a state of "wanting to run without running" and "wanting to jump without jumping" by solely seeking its purpose without the corresponding consequence. During the exercise, the heel is slightly lifted and the sole of the foot is touching the ground with only one part being in contact with the floor.

The triangular zone 1-2-3-4 of the foot is described in the drawing above:

1. Support point
2. Energy-release point
3. "Stretching-tightening" point
4. "Rubbing-flattening" point

This reduced surface supports the entire weight of the body. We train to reinforce the force of this pressure on the selected areas. After much training, gradually going from the bottom to the top, we are able to connect all the body parts, even distinguishing the bone from muscle at times and perform "Contraction/Relaxation" without using the bone in order to succeed in attaining a level characterized by:

- All the body parts being connected from the top to the bottom
- The muscles of the body being united
- The entire action of the "Contraction/Relaxation" being done in one action
- Having the possibility of releasing energy in an extremely short time
- Having the possibility of continued energy-release controlled

by volume

The level of difficulty of "Contraction/Relaxation" that can generally be mastered is described in the following ascending order: buttock and thigh; leg; foot, with the most difficult being the foot. This physical phenomenon must be taken into consideration and one must concentrate solely on nerve endings and tendons with the aim of training for movement in this area. In this way, a solid base is built for a strong reflex action. Once the movement method is formed, it slowly develops from the bottom to the top and successively continues to achieve a level of uniformity in the muscles at the end.

E. THE MOVEMENT OF RUNNING

The movement of running is designed to train "Contraction/Relaxation" in the foot is identified by seeking the cause of the movement and not the consequence, by beginning the phase of running by using applied strength from behind pushing downwards.

Generally, the preparation to begin running is a transitory action that is done by pushing against the floor with the sole of the foot at first and then raising the feet to start to run. Therefore, the first action is the cause and the second action is the consequence. The exercise of Standing Like a Tree in an upright position without moving is defined by seeking the cause without the consequence i.e. pushing against the floor without lifting the feet to run. We only aim to produce the cause of the "Contraction/Relaxation" movement by using the foot's pressure without having the consequence of the "foot being raised". The sole of the foot stays in permanent contact with the floor. This exercise is a form of mental training used to change the system of movement and create the extraordinary method of Yi Quan (or Da Cheng Quan).

Its position can be described as follows: the two feet are separated shoulder width apart, the heels are slightly lifted off the floor and the sole of the foot remains in contact with the floor supporting the body's centre of gravity. Without moving the knees vertically or horizontally the body remains still. Imagine the beginning of a race: the short-term action of pushing against the floor with the soles of the feet without raising them. Alternately, the left foot is in action while the right one is at rest or the two work at the same time until a type of fatigue is felt in the legs' muscles. Be very careful when using the "Contraction/Relaxation" force in the leg muscles at rest as well as the ones on at work, while getting ready to "run" without actually running. For beginners, coordination between the brain's instruction and movement in the sole of the feet is perhaps difficult because of the useless utilisation of strength or the inhomogeneity of the two feet. However, gradually with continued practice, these actions can be independently controlled.

## F. THE MOVEMENT OF JUMPING

The movement of jumping aims to train the two sides of the soles of the feet and to master the way of "Contraction/Relaxation" by wanting to jump, powered by the applied strength, but not jumping.

Its position is done in the following way: First, place both the feet shoulder width apart. Then, imagine the action of jumping that is made up of an action of "Contraction/Relaxation" in the muscles in the part of the legs and soles of the feet, that push against the floor with all the body's strength. Once again, we try to produce the cause without the consequence of the jump i.e. the sole of the foot pushes against the ground without being raised. After this, try to stay still as mush as possible without moving. Repeating this several times, this movement can be done either with both the feet at the same time or alternately with the left foot then the right. Gradually, increase the pressure applied and the jump, being careful to maintain the initial position of the knees; meaning that only the foot and leg's resting muscles contract and relax whilst the other parts of the body are at rest.

## G. THE MOVEMENT OF "STRETCHING / TIGHTENING"

The movement of "Stretching/Tightening" consists in training the action of "Contraction/Relaxation" by using the strength from "Stretching/Tightening" in the muscles and nerves of the foot.

The position is the following: place both the two feet shoulder width apart; the knees are slightly bent; the sole of the foot is touching the floor; the heels are just slightly raised; keep the feet as parallel as possible.

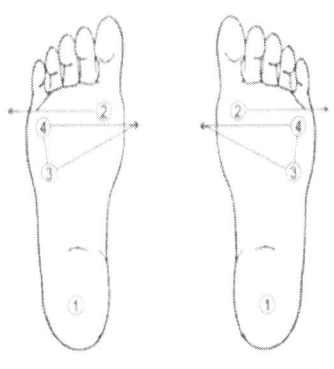

Position of the feet

Apply the strength of "stretching/twisting" outwards on the two soles of the feet at the points of energy-release while maintaining the position of the knees without moving or turning inwards. Use the strength of "pulling/tightening" as well for points 3 and 4: "Stretching/Tightening" and "Rubbing/Flattening". At the same time, slightly push (stretch) the knees towards the outside, pull the leg and thigh muscles from the top and tighten the buttocks inwards while raising the anus. Be sure not to hold your breath. Continue this movement of foot "Contraction/Relaxation", "Stretching/Twisting" outwards and "Stretching/Tightening" until it is no longer possible to do so. An area of 2-5 mm of foot movement is suitable.

The method above is difficult to carry out until the end at the beginning. Beginners can limit themselves to foot movement only to start and then, apply it to other parts of the legs, thighs and buttocks.

## H. THE MOVEMENT OF "SLIDING / STOPPING"

The movement of "Sliding / Stopping" consists in training the action of "Contraction-Relaxation", while sliding and stopping the muscles of the soles of the feet in front and behind on the ground.

The feet are in a V position as indicated below with one foot in front and the other behind. The two heels are slightly raised without touching the ground. The knee in front is somewhat pushed forward. The two legs are pulled by tightening in an upward position.

Body weight is distributed at 40% in front and 60% behind. The mind instructs the sole of the foot in front to strongly but slowly slide forward while the sole of foot behind slides in the same way in the opposite direction and vice versa, in such a way, so that r the respective directions of both the feet are opposite.

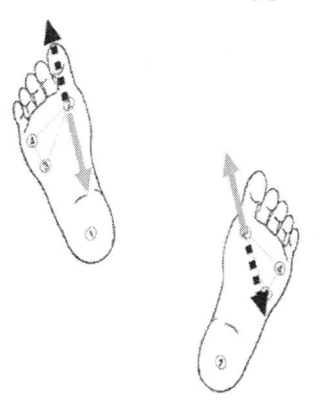

In this way, by alternately changing the movements of both the feet, we move from the action of "Contraction / Relaxation" to "Sliding / Cutting" until you feel tired. The area of movement is between 2mm and 5mm. With much training, we are able to feel a sort of resistance like when filing iron.

## I. THE MOVEMENT OF "CRUSHING / RUBBING"

The action of crushing relates to the pressure exerted on the ground. Rubbing relates to rubbing the sole of the foot in front with force.

The same position is used for the feet where one is in front and the other is behind with the two heels slightly lifted without touching the ground. The knee in front is slightly pushed forward. The muscles in both the legs and thighs are stretched while tightening in an upward position. While establishing the position, the mind instructs the sole of the foot behind to flatten and push against the floor while the sole of the foot in front is instructed to rub once in the forward / downward direction. The two actions are applied with strength. In the same way, the sole of the foot in front rubs backwards while the one behind crushes / pushes once by pulling and tightening the leg and thigh. In this way, the movements of "Crushing / Rubbing" are repeated by the soles of the feet while pulling and tightening the legs and thighs.

## J. THE MOVEMENT OF "PULLING / LIFTING"

The movement of "Pulling / Lifting" is also known as the Movement of Bone Liberation or the Method of "Contraction / Relaxation" of Liberation of the Bone or the Uniform Method of Liberation of the Bone and Rubbing of the Tendon. This movement is the continuation of methods that allows how to master running, jumping, pushing, rubbing, flattening, tightening, sliding and cutting movements with ease by the actions of the sole of the foot. In this movement the lower tendons are connected with the legs and thigh muscles to create two flexible rubber cords that separate the corresponding bones. In this situation of separation of the muscles and bones, we practise the movement of "Contraction / Relaxation" in a uniform way by "Pulling / Lifting".

During the exercise the two feet should form a V-shape. The support point is the triangular zone of the sole of the foot. Strength is applied from the leg, then thigh, then buttocks and kidneys via the stomach (which is considered the central point of the axis), and then towards the chest, back, shoulder, neck and then to the elbow and hand. Altogether, it creates two flexible rubber cords. Depending on the axis of the kidney-stomach-hip, the mind commands the creation of a uniform movement in the three directions of "Pulling/Lifting", "Crushing/Rubbing", "Stretching/Tightening" as well as "Contraction/Relaxation" from pulling the tendon etc. I consider this type of practice as a method to distinguish the bones from the muscles and to unify all the parts of the muscles to carry out the movement of "Pulling/Lifting" and call it the Method of "Contraction/Relaxation" of Bone Liberation. This strength is applied with the intention of competing with the universe.

# CHAPTER VI
# A STUDY ON QI (ENERGY)

## 1. WHAT IS QI?

Since ancient times, Qi has been named differently in the domain of martial arts. For example: Real Qi, Original Qi, Pure Qi, Internal and External Qi, etc. These unclear and mysterious names are difficult to adapt to modern science. Where do we find Real Qi and Original Qi according to the principles of medicine, physics, chemistry and biology? The domain of Qi would have to be modernized in order to study it with scientific methods and describe it in a language that is comprehensible.

Precautions will therefore be necessary to take in order to consider the complexity of the study. Moreover, partial results for measurements by modern instruments on the External Qi cannot be immediately understood as a qualitative property. For example, certain External Qi's are shown in the form of an infra-red wave. It is much more complex and one cannot simply analyses Qi by mixed effects of physics and chemistry. Until now, we have been able to test certain measurable effects of Qi but are not yet able to understand it as a qualitative form. Reasoning with false effects must also be avoided.

What really is Qi? Until now, there is no one theory. Certain interpretations and effects need thorough studies. Names printed in scientific press or philosophy are too simple. They add to the confusions of language that already exist in science or philosophy and especially in medicine. Following are some examples.

## A. QI IS A MAGNETIC WAVE

It has been published in the press that Qi is a magnetic wave without any solid information on theory or practice. It is also said that the length of the wave can even be measured in micrometers. This statement is too vague, unreliable and obviously creates debates in the science sector.

It is true that measurement tools on the magnetic waves are able to observe phenomena in Qi but it is distorted to then say that Qi is a magnetic wave. To prove this, there would need to be more dedicated work.

Many phenomena show the difference between Qi and a magnetic wave. For example, a magnetic wave cannot penetrate sheet metal while Qi can easily do so. Furthermore, Qi can move slowly whilst a magnetic wave always moves at the speed of light. It is therefore irresponsible to say that Qi is a magnetic wave.

## B. QI IS A LOW FREQUENCY INFRA-RED WAVE

In 1978 at the Shanghai Institute of Nuclear Research, Mr. Guo Han Shen, using a device for measuring infra-red rays that he himself developed, was able to receive infra-red waves emitted by Master Hou Sheng Lin. This was released by External Qi with his concentration on his Lao Gong Xue acupuncture point on the left hand at a distance of 1.2 cm. The same result was observed by Master Guang Chao in 1979 in Beijing. Since then, we have believed that Qi is a type of infra-red wave.

It is too risky to say that Qi is an infra-red wave just because it sometimes appears in this form. Qi can also be tested by a measuring tool for static electricity. Can we then say that Qi is a form of static electricity and not an infra-red wave?

Consequently, it is untrue to say that Qi is an infra-red wave. This is a partial description of the phenomenon because only an opposite demonstration is needed to prove the contrary. To do this, an infra-red wave can be emitted on a device for static electricity measurement in order to observe if this artificial Qi can act or not. The obvious result shows the contrary.

These trials can surely be extended by adding several sources of electromagnetic waves, neutrons etc. and numerous measures to block certain waves. The same result will not be achieved with just one Qi.

We can conclude by saying that the study on Qi has to be carried out in a dedicated manner removing all inappropriate definitions.

## C. QI'S FIELD

During a Seminar of Modernisation of Traditional Medicine at the Institute of Research for Aerospace Medicine, Mr. Xue Shen Qian, a well-known scientific researcher said "Some people who agree with the theory of field, introduce the notion of field every time we are not able to present a phenomenon in Chinese medicine.

They therefore create fields of the body, of Qi etc. Based on what founding principles do they create all these fields? Perhaps in their imagination. The proper way to research is not by explaining things according to theories of imaginary fields. Because at the end, that doesn't solve the problem. Let us hope that these persons will change their method and not try to understand something unknown by something else that is unknown."

Despite everything, a Master who practises Qi respects biological human law. He cannot jump higher than 2.42 m while respecting the law of the strength of gravity; he cannot run 100 m in faster than 9.83 sec. while respecting the law of momentum.

Someone practising the "iron shirt" is still unable to withstand a gunshot. He is fully human made with proteins but just capable of withstanding more strength than other normal people. Since Qi respects the laws of science and modern medicine, it is necessary and possible to understand it by scientific method.

In Russia, after an interview with a manager at a laboratory for electronic and radio tests that carry out long-distance research on biological phenomena observation, a journalist wrote an article entitled "Centre of Scientific Control" in the Science and Life review which stated:

"The laboratory was created in 1982, at the time when everyone was speaking about phenomena linked to special abilities. Many people were interested in the topic and were waiting on explanations – proof. Exaggerated examples of diagnostics and healing were being spoken of without concrete results. The laboratory decided to study these phenomena by applying methods of physics and radiology in order to look for proof. Seven methods were used:

- Increase in temperature on the surface with infra-red wave radiation;
- Change in temperature on the inside of the body due to the radiation of the radio wave;
- Electric field;
- Chemical radiation;
- Sound wave;
- Chemical combination released by the skin in the form of vapor and aerosol.

First of all, the word "special" in the expression "special abilities" is unsuitable because with the seven methods listed above and all the persons studied, not much difference was found. Only minor heat from thermal radiation that was released by the hand had been detected.

Researchers believe that the magnetic field created by the body only respects a percentage of one over one million. As a result, it is not likely that the body will create an equal magnetic effect.

The sensation of heating has to be tested on the skin by the electric method. It represents about 0.1 mm $W/cm^2$, the equivalent of receiving heat from a matchstick at a distance of one metre.

Between certain organs and the body's skin, there are bonds controlled by the central nervous system. As such, from one area on the skin (considered as the body's window) we can observe the body. Through it, we can even have certain influences on the body e.g. heat on the skin to incite the functioning of the corresponding organs.

Question: Is it possible for a person to have an effect on another through thermal effect?

*Response*: Average thermal radiation in the body is at around 100 W. Distributed in an equal manner on the body, the part on the hand represents 0.1 W. It is not insignificant as after all, we are able to feel heat from a distance of 20 to 30 cm. In fact, the hand can feel a difference in temperature of 0.3 degrees at a short distance.

People who have "special abilities" gather information and then treat illnesses, most likely by means of thermal role.

Question: Is it possible for one person to have an effect on another by means of radio frequency energy?

*Response*: The quantity of radio frequency energy coming out of the body is too small. It would need to be multiplied by 100 million times to see a difference.

Conclusion: We have not discovered special abilities in a biological body. We have only identified the possibility of using thermal role to produce effects on the functioning of the body.

## 2. COMMENTARIES FROM ABROAD

### A. REPORT FROM THE COMMITTEE OF SCIENCE OF THE UNITED STATES

According to a report from Science and Technology Daily on the

29th June 1988: "For years, numerous writings on special abilities have been done issued from government as well as the population. After 130 years of observation, a report conducted by the Committee of Science of the United States has confirmed that the results obtained had to be supported by real and indisputable experiments. This report has been approved by the Research Commission of the United States.

## B. DISCOVER REPORT

In an article titled "Abuse of the people" of Discover in volume II, 1998, it was written: "One Sunday in April 1986, millions of people were gathered in front of the Furax Church in Detroit. They were waiting for a pastor named Popofu to be miraculously healed. 57 television channels aired the show live during which unbelievable scenes were being watched, such as: the sick throwing away their walking sticks, people crying while screaming etc.

How can this phenomenon be explained?

> It has been proven that if we give a sweet insisting on its efficiency, one third of sick people can confirm feeling a positive effect. This represents a typical case of the method of suggestion. The same principle can explain the effect caused by a man considered to have special abilities just by touching the forehead of another person with his hand.

> We can suspect cheating with the help of accomplices.

> Mr. James Landi is a professional magician. Since the year 1975, equipped with audiovisual instruments, he has been revealing this type of cheating. He went to the scene as well and with the help of his assistant, discovered how Popofu was able to say the exact name, address and disease of a person selected amongst the

billions of unknown people. His wife chatted with the people and he heard the conversation at the same time. After this discovery, the pastor was obligated to close his head office. Despite this demonstration, it is still difficult to persuade everyone to believe that paranormal strength does not exist, most importantly, when we are sick and will do whatever it takes to be healed.

## 3. TEST OF EXTERNAL QI

### A. EFFECTS OF EXTERNAL QI

External Qi, so to say, is released by the bodies of well-practised individuals. Persons who release Qi still use means such as certain gestures, words, actions or suggestions; otherwise there is no effect. When a believer is in front of someone who releases Qi, he/she is influenced by his gesture and allows himself to develop certain psychological and physical changes that create different sensations. Without this belief and without knowing that he has been trained to receive this Qi, there can be no effect. As such, if the eyes of believers are blindfolded, blocking the passage of information, or if one is not a believer in external Qi, a negative result is produced on the release of Qi.

After analyzing, the effect of external Qi is nothing but the result of suggestion and hypnotism.

# CHAPTER VII
# A STUDY ON THE "OBJECT"

## 1. WHAT IS THE "OBJECT"?

In the article titled "Precise History of the Theory of Qi Gong at the Beginning of the Qin Era" published in the review, *China Qi Gong* N° 4 1985, Mr. Liu AnFeng and Mr. Zhang Guangbe showed their understanding of a writing by Guanzi and indicated that "According to the Theory of Rest, one must "observe before moving because movement alters position whilst resting maintains it by itself."—Guanzi. This means that one must avoid external influences and not be bothered by positive or negative personal feelings in order to stay calm".

I do not share the same point of view as Mr. Liu and Mr. Zhang and wish to share some of my opinions to debate with them.

Firstly, I believe that the sentence quoted above is not linked to the notion of "Rest" but to the method of finding the "Object". In this sentence, movement means shifting and Rest means "staying still" in a relative sense and not in the sense of "going into rest" (mentally).

The word "Object" occupies the most important place in the comprehension of the sentence. One must capture the real sense in order to understand.

Here are the interpretations that I offer on the readings of Guanzi.

The four limbs cannot work if the brain diverts from the principle of the doctrine of Tao which is: not exhausting the horse by making it run too fast; not damaging the wings by making birds fly; activating the body only after having obtained the "object" in order to observe the rule of change in itself (otherwise we loose the position specific to the "object" by moving); it is only in standing still that we can achieve the "object".

This principle is found in another sentence by Guanzi: The reasons for not moving before achieving the "object" are: the brain cannot stay calm when the upper and lower body are moving by wavering or jumping. That is to say, the limbs being in movement interrupt the brain from observing the rule of change in the "object". Secondly, position means "without moving". Thirdly, by standing still without moving, we can avoid wavering or trembling. To summarize, we can achieve the "object" by standing still.

According to the quotations above, one can assume that:

Moving is the equivalent of a horse walking, of a bird flying, swinging which is the state of a person who is not calm or an activity of shifting. However, Rest means "standing still" and does not mean entering into a state of Rest.

Guanzi has clearly indicated that these movements of the horse, of the bird, of swinging and of non-tranquility all divert from the Tao. Only "Observe before moving" is correct. Unfortunately, few people know this principle and try to learn the movements of a horse, of a bird, of swinging and of non-tranquility against the real Tao. Therefore, how can one achieve the "Object" with observing these rules?

But what is this "Object"?

"Object is something that is characterized by all that has an appearance, sound, image and color. It is independent of our mind. Many forms of movement exist in our unified and complete body. Some are controlled by the system of first signals. Men, like animals, are born with them. On the other hand, another part of the movements controlled by the system of second signals is developed through learning, training and fine tuning after birth. This state of high-class movement characterized by non-stop and complete series like an art is called "Object" or "Thing". It is also called "Strength" or "Martial Arts Strength" or "Strength Release". The clear difference between martial arts and conventional sports is in the research of this "Object". As the grand master Wang Xiangzhai said, "The art of learning is not knowing how to do a gesture or a series of gestures".

The importance lies in mastering the "Object."

Laozi said: "the "Object" has always existed." It is impossible that it has disappeared since man exists. The problem is how to learn it, apply it and develop it because its knowledge is taught by humans. It represents a state of mind that one cannot imitate by pretending (this can be seen by just looking) but it is difficult to describe. It is beyond the mechanical domain, the body reaches a level where it unifies shape, strength, energy and physiognomy. It manifests under the aspect of something spectacular, of well-trained muscles and skilful action. The "Object" is not something to be bought with money, a gift to be given or something that is inherited. Laozi therefore said: "If the Tao is given, it belongs to the heads of State, close relatives, brother and descendants." Man must obtain it through study and training, according to the principle of Tao.

The great master Wang Xiangzhai, inventor of Da Cheng, reformer and theorist of martial arts, wrote in his book "Principles of martial arts", in point 9 of the general principle: "We can seek the 'Object' if we distance from ourselves, we will find nothing if we remain ourselves". He also separates the "object" into two parts, internal and external, and gives proof of the real existence of the "Object".

This conclusion has been made after having studied all theories of martial arts in detail, from the mechanics of the body to those concerning the mind, and also through practice on strength techniques and real attacks, in order to master the true "Object".

## 2. THE OBJECT DESCRIBED BY LAOZI

Laozi wrote:

> The "Object" is not visible,
> it is said to be "colorless";
> we cannot hear it,
> it is said to be "soundless";
> we cannot touch it,

it is said to be "shapeless";
we cannot seek out its cause too much,
the three are something at its origin,
it is not shiny on top,
nor dark below,
endless, without rigidity, without explanation,
in the end, it goes back to the original state of nothingness,
a shape without a fixed shape,
an aspect without an object,
it is vague,
without a head in front,
without a tail behind.

As the "Object" does not have any fixed shape; it has an aspect of action experienced by someone who possesses this high class virtue from training. This form of action is different from a normal gesture that can only be observed when it is expressed. Therefore, "the 'Object' in itself" is not visible, audible or touchable."

| Laozi | Wang Xiangzhai |
| --- | --- |
| Person skilled in Tao | |
| Fine and intelligent | |
| Very profound and difficult to recognise | |
| One describes it with difficulty | |
| Prudent like when walking on fine glass | To walks like a cat and vigilant like a monkey |
| Vigilant of enemy attacks | To release strength and keep the mind-like hair that stand up like halberds |
| Modest and serious | Behaves with respect, modesty and prudence |
| Like a guest | Like someone who attends a banquet |
| Behaves kindly and harmoniously to melt glass | To fill the body with emptiness and to have a clear mind so that not a feather can stick to the body |

| | |
|---|---|
| Simple and honest like un-carved wood | Form like water that flows, empty like air |
| Empty and vast like a calm valley of an immense mountain | Respect that allows to fill filling the prudent mind like in front of a deep gorge |
| Innocent and simple | To kill all different ideas |
| Like troubled water | Immobile and concentrates as if to listen to the sound of drizzles |
| Silent and light like the deep sea, like a theft without attachment | In a spiritual activity, moves like a mountain that flies and concentrates its strength like water that flows |
| as though it was endless | A light contact is enough to start the action, continuous explosion |

Relations between Qi (Energy), Strength, Object and Tao

## 3. RELATIONS BETWEEN QI (ENERGY), STRENGTH, OBJECT AND TAO

The "Object" is the Qi in "Qi Gong". All the phenomena of Qi during the exercise, considered as inevitable biological relations, are included in the quest for the "Object". Studies of Qi as well as corresponding books are abundant in history but many are based on superstition. Many participants coming from intellectual environments are incapable of freeing themselves from this phase of blind belief. Likewise, in martial arts, we consider this phenomenon as "Strength". In Tai Chi, one talks about listening, understanding, diverting, directing, launching, etc., the Strength.

The great master, Wang Xiangzhai, attached great importance to the quest for the "Object". He required that students be able to "observe the "Object" by "leaving a mark on the outside of the body", with each gesture and not make empty movements without the "Object". To be able to search for the "Object" better, he insisted on a standing position without moving. He said: "To be able to know the truth, start by Standing Like a Tree; look for rapid action in immobility; look for strength in the absence of strength: look for skill in clumsiness; look for difference in indifference." He also added: "It is better to do small actions than big ones or immobile ones instead of small ones as the action of immobility is in continuous movement."

- Do not move without having found the "Object".
- Observe and test the law of development of the "Object" in a fixed position.

The "Object" is lost if movement is too early before having truly acquired it. After several years of experience, we cannot obtain the "Object" through practice in movement. A considerable amount of time must be spent in the practice of not moving to be able to reach to that stage.

Laozi said: "Tao (law) created the Object, De (Virtue) conserves it: the "Object" represents Tao and De and shapes them".

But what is this "Object"?

"It is created by gesture." The "object" is introduced in multiple gestures. People gifted for showing it in the form of a gesture are called "gifted people of Tao" by Laozi. Below are some sentences from Laozi and Wang Xiangzhai:

## 4. TO FORGET WHILE IN A SEATED POSITION AND TO CREATE IN TAO

"Enter into silence" is only the beginning of the practice. It represents the process of control in the brain. It is quite effective for healing, especially for the elderly and physically weak people. One may even cure certain illnesses. Secondly, in the higher stage of training, it is important to look for agitation in the brain. This is the step for the quest of the "Object". All the difference between martial arts, Standing Like a Tree, Qi Gong and sports is this: In sports we look for speed, strength and external beauty without giving enough importance to internal development of the body i.e. the "Object".

One of the Kongzi students, Yan Hui, said before: Forgetting while in a seated position means leaving the arms and legs free, removing intelligence, distancing from shape and removing knowledge to get to the higher stage of intelligence." (Zhuangzi) This is exactly the result reflecting the situation where the brain has reached its highest point of control. At this level, participants are quite satisfied with the result. We can thus say that even the great scholar, Kongzi, is not at the highest level since he does not know how to explain what is "forgetting while in a seated position" to his student, Yan Hui.

On the contrary, another great scholar, Guangzi, said: "Do not move before obtaining the "Object", observe the rules; if we move, we lose our position, the opposite leads to us keeping it." In this aspect, Guangzi seems to have more insight than Kongzi.

In China, in the oldest book of Medicine, The Laws of Emperor Huang, it was written:

"I heard of a true man in history who was so strong that he could lift the sky and move the earth, control Yin and Yang, breathe the energy of air; focus his mind and unify his muscles. All of this allowed him to live as long as nature. He was the living Tao."— Emperor Huang

"Lifting the sky and moving the earth" does not mean that someone can lift the sky and move the earth. It expresses a mental activity of supposition and the way of doing (pretending). This expression is exaggerated to intensify the mind's concentration by imagining that one is lifting the sky and moving the earth.

The modern terminology used by Standing Like a Tree is: carry on the head; carry on the shoulders; pull with one's hands; step over with legs; surround with the body.

In "Controlling Yin and Yang" it is not the Yin and Yan related to the five main elements that describe the rules of the universe; we can consider them as the mechanical rules that control the body in movement i.e. the rule of change in Yin (empty) and Yang (full) related to the muscular movements in the body during the practice of attack techniques.

"Breathing energy from air" means breathing in fresh air—training in a place where there is fresh air.

"Focusing one's mind" is a method of training the body of a real man that is equal to the practice described by Laozi called living Tao. In history, Standing Like a Tree was created from this. All types of martial arts start by practising Posture a Tree.

"Unifying the muscles" means that after a long period of training with a strong concentration of the mind, the body's muscles are controlled by the nerves, coordination is expanded and the body is more unified. Although the body is made up of 639 muscles, we can coordinate them as though it was only one unit in movement. In terms of posture, we describe it as "complete"; all the difference between real men and ordinary men can be found in this. The method of "pretending" was given in heritage to the modern practice of Standing Like a Tree.

Through these five short sentences mentioned above, we can observe a certain level on the experiences and theories of our ancestors in martial arts and techniques for preserving health. They were able to live longer after having understood these laws.

## 5. THE MOST IMPORTANT USE OF THE "OBJECT"

In order to prove the very existence of the characteristics and roles of the "Object, not only by definitions of Laozi or to show that it is not a pure invention, we show the following correspondence between in quotations of Laozi and the principles of Yi Quan:

"Action and the way of man having great morality"

It closely follows Tao (principle of life).

> "Tao is something without a fixed shape
> different and similar,
> although fundamentally there is some shape,
> there is something real.

> it is so profound and unclear
> but very refined
> and it is so real
> that in technique we count on this sort of highly refined
> "Object"
> when faced with attack."

How do we verify the effectiveness of this method when faced with an attack? Laozi also wrote:

> "We speak of the man who has reached a high level
> in the study of Tao.
> He is not afraid of bulls or tigers
> when he passes close by.
> He is not injured during war.
> Why is the bull no longer able
> to attack with its horns?
> And the tiger with its paws?
> And the enemy with his weapons.
> Because he has mastered the "Object",
> that allows him to fight his adversary without being harmed."

## 6. THE "OBJECT" OF YI QUAN

The "Object" in Yi Quan is strength (strength in martial arts or strength release etc.) developed by training in Posture a Tree, strength-testing and strength release. This strength is called "Thing". These three aspects each have a form of expression in which, according to the corresponding gestures, two types can be distinguished: "with the object" and "without the object". The first can also be partially, completely, internally or externally distinguished from the body. For example, training where one practises with flexible actions, of connections or pulling the tendon etc., which consist in practising wih natural strength, relaxing without letting go, squeezing without stiffening, relaxing the shape and concentrating the mind etc. All of this aims to develop the inside of the body. We can also say "It belongs to the part of the body without an object." Although the aspects are abstract, in practices such as lifting the sky and moving the earth, mastering Yin and Yang, moving like a flying mountain, staying calm like a river that flows etc., when we get to a certain level, the body goes beyond the mechanical domain and creates an inner transformation. At this time, we notice a sense of internal grandeur in the body that searches for the "thing" on the outside of the body.

The permanent quest for the "Object" in martial arts in China means going to the depths of the mind, from the inside to the outside, gradually, from the bottom to the top and thus goes from a change in quantity to a change in quality. If we limit ourselves to the inside of the body, we will never get to the level characterized by "release as soon as we touch" and "all over the body like an elastic spring".

I call all the expressions of "Object", of "Thing" and of "Strength", "the secondary voluntary movement".

# CHAPTER VIII
# THE QUEST FOR THE "OBJECT"
# THROUGH STANDING LIKE A TREE

## 1. CATEGORIZING OF THE "OBJECT"

In China's history, the methods of training to live better are: Tao; Medicine; Confucianism; Tao Religion and; Buddhism. It was only in these modern times that Martial Arts, Internal Gong (energy), External Gong, Gong of the air, Standing Like a Tree, etc. were developed. According to the normal belief, Laozi (571-471 BC) was the founder of Tao. The Tao religion has its roots in China and it originates from ancient witchcraft. It is different to the Tao philosophy inspired by thought. In 142 in the Province of Si Chan region under the Dong Han Dynasty, Zhang Tao Ling created the practice of the Tao religion. They asked everyone who wanted to practise the religion to contribute five sacks of rice. This is where the name "religion of five sacks of rice" came from. They named Laozi, father of the religion and "great sovereign". They also chose the book, Laozi, as one of their bibles. However, in truth and in fact, the Tao philosophy and the Tao religion are not one and the same thing.

In the book, Guangzi, published one hundred years before Laozi, the notions about Tao (principle), De (morality), Wu (object) and Qi (energy) were already present. However, in history, researchers only concentrated on literary sentences and not on notions other than words (on the human body, for example). The notions corresponding to the sentences: not moving before obtaining the "Object" (Guangzi); "standing without moving" (Laozi) and concentrating one's mind (Principles of Huang Di) are now called Standing Like a Tree in quest of the "Object".

According to Guangzi, each object has a characteristic, such as a name that cannot be discovered without a quest (Guangzi). There are many studies on "Tao", "De" and "Qi" but not enough on the "Object". This is shown by the numerous stories that have been written on the "External Object" with very little on the "Internal Object"; the numerous explanations about its philosophic side with little on longevity practices and the numerous books have been written by authors who do not know nor master the "Object". Actually, very few people master it. Many explanations have been given with old theories. Very little explanations have been given with modern notions. All of this leads to a false understanding of the notion of the "Object". In fact Tao is the same as Wu (object). The first is theory, principle and method. The second is the aspect that shows the first on the human body and not on the general notion of the object in the universe. We can understand this general notion on the body in two sections. The first, as with everything in the world, has a shape and is the "External Object" that appears at birth. The second is shapeless and does not appear at birth according to Laozi and is called the "Internal Object".

"Create without having" (Laozi) has been understood in several ways such as "create and remove all things without having them". Guoli (Story of Laozi) understands "to have" as "to possess". Supposing that "Tao" creates all things; then "De" nurtures them. However, that does not signify possessing them. I think that "not having" signifies "having". "Having" is the state of existing. "Not having" is the state of not existing. Without having what? Without having a fixed object. For example, the sensations of aches, pins and needs, vibration or cold and heat at the start of Posture a Tree are objects without a shape "we are not able to see, hear or touch" (Laozi). After the exercise, "everything reduces to nothing" (Laozi). This sensation of "creating without having" or "Internal Object" is understood as "Qi (air)" or the "Qi sensation". This develops from the initial sensation and turns into an ache, then into an uneasy feeling or cold and heat etc. It is as if "Tao created 1, 1 creates 2, 2 creates 3 and 3 creates all the other things" (Laozi) and is the same for Tao used to increase the longevity by practising Zhan Zhuang (see Chapter 1: Reactions of the Body After Practice).

Internal objects such as aches, pins and needles, vibration and sensations of hot and cold are the opposite of external objects such as those present in nature: the sun, the moon, the stars, the sea, the mountains, the trees, the animals as well as planes, buildings, money etc. made by man. The first set of objects are shapeless and are considered as "creating without having". The second set is objects that have shapes and are considered as "creating and having". We can conclude by saying that "creating without having" in the sense of Standing Like a Tree means creating and nurturing something having a fixed shape i.e. aches, pins and needles, feeling uneasy "that we cannot see, hear or touch". Specific internal objects gradually transform from the bottom to the top and from quantitative to qualitative in a recurring manner. That is to say, "growing them and nurturing them" (Laozi) as well as "all the things in nature produce and ripen" (Laozi). Then, they are "nurtured and observed" (Laozi). At the end, through the practice of Qi Gong, we achieve a level of "Tao practice" (Laozi).

As such, after showing a state of mind of "walking on fine glass, vigilant of enemy attacks", "lifting the sky, moving the earth, controlling Yin and Yang", "anticipating without being noticed, following behind without finding the line", "everything goes back to nothingness" (see table on the following page).

The difference between "Wu (Object)" and "Qi (energy)" is that Qi is the sensation felt by the body of all beginners at the beginning of the practice. We can thus say that Qi is a feeling within itself that is subjective, empty and invisible while the "Object" is a state of mind shown only by participants who have a certain level that cannot be attained without special study and rigorous practice. Therefore, the "Object" is an objective, concrete, realistic and visible expression. Learning martial arts means studying Tao (principle of life) in which the aim is the quest for the "Object". As Master Wang Xiangzhai said "Distancing oneself from the body without a quest for object, one is never successful". This sentence is key in Da Cheng Quan. I believe that in order to really understand the Tao described by Laozi in training for improving health, one would need to begin by understanding the notion of "Object". It is only at a high level of training when the body already possesses the "Object", as Laozi said "practising Tao, appearing to be a great connoisseur and understanding the principle of life", that we are really able to understand the notions of Tao (Laws and Principles), De (Virtue and Morality), Wu (Object) and Qi (Energy) after having compared these notions. We are also able to acquire a profound understanding of the Tao method of exercise as well as the 5000 character-long notes in Laozi concerning the principle of life and training.

## Object

### With the Body as a Barrier

| External | Internal |
| --- | --- |
| Objects outside the body possessed from birth | Objects on the inside of the body that are not possessed at birth |
| I – Objects in nature, sun, moon, star, earth, mountain, valley, sea, wind, rain, thunder, animals, plants, relaxation, concentrated mind ; uniformed muscles ; looking without being found ; obtaining without taking, everything returns to nothingness. | I – Subjective objects such as pins and needles, aches, coldness, heat, fatigue, sleepiness, light, well-being, ; relaxing without letting go, contracting without being rigid, shape. |
| II – Man-made objects, nuclear weapons, planes, canons, buildings, money, gold, treasures, inside there is the Object and the Image ; Image without object has a shape, each shape has a name ; how to get to know another without understanding oneself. | II – Objective objects shown " walking on very fine glass, vigilant of enemy attacks. " "Lifting the sky, moving the earth and controlling Yin and Yang". |

Categories of Objects

Writing is the symbol of saving and transferring expressions of language. This tool allowing to enhance exchange by language participates thus, in the development of human civilization. We define illiterate people by those not knowing how to read or write. Can we attribute the same sense to our domain of people not knowing the "Object" or "Tao"? We spend time learning how to read and write. The most difficult is the classic language as a conception of the "Object" etc. In acknowledgement of the "Object", Laozi says this one is a symbol of expression of Tao and De. It comes from "being born with, creating without having, looking without being found, listening without being heard, obtaining without taking." It is therefore "the state without a state, the image without object, stunned, moving forward without being seen and following behind without a trace." (Laozi) At the end, everything returns to nothingness" (Laozi). This is a hidden ability possessed by all men and common in all and is kept "from ancient times until now, forever" (Laozi). This is very useful for man, allowing him to develop his mind, abilities or reinforce his health. This thus, explains the main difference between the two completely different methods, Standing Like a Tree and conventional sports today. At the same time, just as doing beautiful calligraphy takes time, no one can obtain the "Object" without practising a special method for a long time.

The symbols of writing are different according to the regions of the country but the ones for the "Object" are unique and remain unchanged with a certain norm where every participant practising Standing Like a Tree shows the same aspect of the "Object". There is only a difference in the degree of mastery. It is unfortunate that in history we were only able to write a few words about the "Object" without any photos about its characteristics. It is thus impossible for people to possess the real "Object" and understand the real sense through these writings that have undergone several modifications. Today, with the use of modern means, we can keep it forever with the help of photos, videocassettes or cinema etc. We can compare it, study it and admire it. We are able to find two contrastinf states between having the "Object" and not having it at all, by comparing photos.

## 2. TAO METHOD

Concerning the historical originality of Standing Like a Tree, it is believed that it was created during the Song Dynasty by General, Fei Yue, who became very well-known after the Jin invasion. He created "Martial Arts in six steps and in mind concentration". However, in reality, it dates further back, in 2700 B.C. during the time of Chun Qiu. In olden stories, it was not called "Standing Like a Tree" nor "Qi Gong" or "Martial Arts". In ancient times, there were always two ways to train to preserve health; one was active and the other was static. The first consisted in moving the limbs of the body e.g. the flight of birds, the walking of horses etc. relative to certain movements. In the second, one remains still in a seated position or standing in quest for the "Object". The first author who called the theory "the quest for the Object" was Guanzi.

Guanzi was written during the Chun Qiu period by a politician, very popular at that time, called Mr. Zhong Guan (730-645 B.C.) His theory, developed afterwards by other people in his name, covers many domains in astrology, economics, agriculture etc. Amongst his stories there is "Xin Shou", "Bai Xin", "Nei Ye" etc. that make reference to the theories of Tao, De, the "Object" and "Qi":

Guanzi:

"If the brain strays from the principle of Tao,
the four limbs will therefore not be able
to move correctly to work;
do not walk like a horse;
do not fly like a bird;
stay still until obtaining the "Object"
(This is the first time it was called "Standing Like a Tree");

in order to observe the internal change in the body;
without which, the "Object" loses its position;
we cannot obtain it only by standing still."

He continues:

"The reasons for staying still without moving the limbs
before obtaining the "Object" are:
the brain cannot be calm if we move;
or if we become impatient;
that is to say that we cannot
observe the rule of change of the "Object"
in the brain if we move our body;
posture means without moving in a standing position;
in this way we are able to obtain the "Object".

Here, Guanzi spoke about the method of practice for the first time in "three no's": do not walk like a horse, do not fly like a bird, do not move. This shows that at the time where practices of walking like a horse and flying like a bird existed (with which Guanzi did not agree) he suggested an opposite method while indicating the disadvantages of this active method.

Other than Guanzi, Laozi has also shown appreciation for the static principle for longevity. Laozi wrote: There is danger if we take the action lightly without knowing the rules." In correlation with the understanding of martial arts and the Guanzi's theory, this means "no positive result will be obtained if we move without knowing the rules of the fixed position". The principle created by Guanzi and Laozi is confirmed by the effective method of Standing Like a Tree.

Laozi (AD 571-471) was one of the most well-known scholars in the Chinese history. He created the theory of Tao. He wrote the Laozi book also under the name of "Principle of Tao and De" in 5000 words which was considered the Tao bible.

After Guanzi, Laozi developed a static theory by explaining his method of practice as well as understandings on expression and the use of the "Object":

> The expression and movement of a great connoisseur of Tao;
> "is based on the study of Tao;
> Tao as an object;
> he is without a fixed aspect, very vague;
> standing still alone;
> in order to observe the magical change;
> on the inside of the body;
> the sensations and reactions continuously circling;
> continues to observe until the end of time.

I chose to put "standing still alone in order to observe the magical change; on the inside of the body; the sensations and reactions continuously circling; he continues to observe until the end of time" together as this explains the principle of Tao.

A good translation of "Standing still alone" is "Alone with the mind concentrated" (principle of Emperor Huang) similar to the sentence "Without moving before in order to obtain the "Object" which shows the same reasoning in another way. All depict the principle of Standing Like a Tree.

## 3. METHOD OF MEDICINE

As with Guanzi and Laozi, there are also signs of the principle of training for health purposes in the Emperor's book, *Principle*. After the book *Story about the History of Chinese Medicine*, *Principle* was written between 450 and 350 B.C.

In the first chapter, it is written:
"Emperor Huang said: I heard of a human being in history who was so strong that he could lift the sky and move the earth, control Yin and Yang, breathe the energy of air; concentrate his mind and

unify his muscles; that he could live as long as nature. He was the living Tao."

There are several understandings of this sentence. In my opinion, seen from the perspective of "Standing Like a Tree", it offers a concrete method of training for health purposes. Here, the human being is someone who masters the method and has attained a high level but still is not considered as a god. The following are detailed interpretations:

—Lifting the sky and moving the earth: not in the literal sense of the words but in a mental activity in the quest for a state of grandeur, in a clear way, this means the head is stretched upwards; the arms are wrapped around the body, the shoulders are lifted; the hands are pulled; the legs are crossed; held tightly by the body. This description is slightly exaggerated in order to train by expanding the mind, imagining being able to life the sky and move the earth.

Controlling Yin and Yang: Here Yin and Yang are not to be taken in the sense of the principle of change of the five elements but in the sense of the rule of the mechanical balance in the body i.e. the principle of change in the muscles in combat techniques.

| Analysis | Original text | Explanation |
| --- | --- | --- |
| Unprecedented mental activity | Lifting the sky and moving the earth; mastering Yin and Yang | • During Standing Like a Tree we carry out a mental activity of lifting the sky and moving the earth;<br>• After a long practice of this exercise, we are able to master the rule of change in the body. |
| Place of exercise | Breathing in the energy of the air | Breathing in air to increase the quantity of air and accelerate circulation in the body. |

| Method of exercise | Standing alone concentrating on the mind | This is the modern Posture of a Tree. |
|---|---|---|
| Result | Muscles unifying | The muscles unify after a long time of exercise, they move as one. |
| Basic theory | Longevity in Tao | This is the result of Tao. |

Analysis of Training Methods

— Breathe in the air's energy: this means choosing an ideal place to do the exercise where fresh air can be inhaled to increase circulation.

— Focus the mind: this is a solid exercise method that is said to be the very basis of training in martial arts.

— Unify the muscles: this means that the muscles, controlled by the nervous system, are able to be coordinated and unified as one through training for a long period of time and concentrating one's mind. Although there are 639 muscles, when they move it should be as if the entire thing was one muscle.

Here, we notice a difference between a great master who can live as long as nature and an ordinary man. This grand master is called the living Tao:

— This sentence symbolizes the words in 51 Laozi: "Tao creates it, De nurtures it, the Object moulds it; tendency makes it a reality."

It can be said that Tao and medical methods are the same. It can even be said that the method of medicine is what created the principle of Tao.

In five sentences we can notice the profound level of theory and practice in the domain of the technique of martial arts and training for health purposes.

Following the analyses stated above and in correlation with the principles of Yi Quan are the following translated sentences:

Emperor Huang said: In ancient times, I heard of a man who trained based on the method of being "alone standing while focusing his mind" in a place where the air was fresh. During the exercise; his mind drifts off and imagines having so much strength that he was able to lift the sky and move the earth. After much practice, the muscles that are controlled by the nervous system are in perfect coordination and unification and move as one. Since this person has perfectly mastered mechanical adjustment in the body as well as combat technique with the change in Yin and Yang (empty and real), he is obviously able to live longer. This is mainly due to the fact that he practised regularly by the principle of "standing alone while focusing his mind". This is what the Tao method for health purposes consists of.

## 4. CONFUCIUS METHOD

As described below, Guanzi said "Do not move before obtaining the Object", Laozi said "Standing still alone while focusing the mind". All of these methods are practised standing. In chapter 6 of Zhuangzi, he describes a conversation between master Kongzi and one of his students, Yan Hui, concerning a method in a seated position:

> "Yan Hui – I've improved.
> Kongzi – How?
> Yan Hui – I have forgotten about routine and pleasure.
> Kongzi – That is good, but it is not enough.
>     ** A few days later **
> Yan Hui – I've improved.
> Kongzi – How?
> Yan Hui – I have forgotten about the virtue of humanity.
> Kongzi – That is good, but it is not enough.
>     ** A few days later **
> Yan Hui – I've improved.
> Kongzi – How?
> Yan Hui – I practise "Forgetting in a seated position".
> Kongzi (Surprised) – What is that?
> Yan Hui – It is forgetting about the limbs;

removing intelligence;
removing basis;
forgetting prior knowledge;
making oneself one with the great Tao,
that is what is "forgetting in a seated position."

This story is represents the first stage, "getting into a calm place", in Standing Like a Tree. It helps with adjustment in the brain and reinforcing physical fitness. In the Chinese history, many writers were happy with themselves to have reached this stage. For example, Su Dong Puo, a great writer from the Northern Song Dynasty said:

"Practising the method in a seated position;
not so significant at the start, but with time
the effect is multiplied;
like taking medication
efficiency is 100 times greater."

In reality, forgetting in a seated position is what results from control in the brain. Another role is excitement. Both are mental activities with the aim of finding the "Object". However, this takes more than just some days. It is difficult to understand and master through simple practice of "forgetting while in a seated position". High-level practice will be needed for lifting the sky, moving the earth, controlling Yin and Yang, focusing the mind independently, unifying the muscles to become one and observing the inner changes in the body.

My teacher, Master Wang Xiangzhai said: "It is absolutely and positively sure that health is improved through practising Standing Like a Tree, but it is difficult to guarantee mastering the Object."

| Tao | Guanzi | Theory of the quest for the object from Guanzi (ref. Chap. VIII-2. Guanzi.) | No movement before obtaining the Object |

|  |  |  |  |
|---|---|---|---|
|  | Laozi | Theory of the quest for the object from Laozi (ref. Chap. VIII-2 Laozi) | Independent without movement |
| Medicine | Chinese Medicine | Theory of survival from Tao (VIII-3) | Independent and focusing on the mind |
| Confucius | Yan Hui | Theory of forgetting while in a seated position (VIII-4) | Forgetting while sitting calmly |
| Tao Religion | Chemistry | • Theory of circulation:<br>• Big Zhou Circulation;<br>• Small Zhou circulation;<br>  Crossing;<br>• Unblocking. | Yin and Yang and eight main elements |
| Buddhism | Dhyana Method | • Theory of dhyana seated;<br>• Crouched position, standing while walking | Symbol and invocation |
| Internal Method | Qi (energy) Method | • Static: expanding, maintaining a vigorous inner activity<br>• Dynamic: five animals, eight ways, muscles | Quest for Qi |
| External Method | Martial Arts | • Series of practice:<br>• South-North;<br>• Interior / Exterior;<br>• Tai Chi, BaGua, XinYi etc. | Quest for strength |

| Standing Like a Tree | • Yi Quan, • Da Cheng Quan | • Theory of DaCheng<br>• Standing Like a Tree;<br>• Inner research of the body; concentrating on oneself; developing the nervous system, distancing from oneself,<br>• Without an object for a quest,<br>• Nothing at all if one does not free himself;<br>• Object = 1st voluntary movement;<br>• (Speed + strength) x time<br>• = 2nd random movement | Quest for the Object |
|---|---|---|---|

Summary of different methods

## 5. TAOISM AND BUDDHISM METHODS

The chemical method (or external tablet) consists in taking tablets to live longer. These tablets are made with products containing mercuric sulphide, sulphur and alum. They dissolve once they are heated and become golden tablets. People believed they would live longer and ascend to heaven after having taken it. In reality, they were mortal poisons.

This practice became popular during the Tang dynasty in the upper class. There were many deaths caused by poison, especially of several well-known emperors.

Li Bai, a great poet at that time who followed Taoism closely in his youth, was also a specialist in this practice. He was fascinated by the research for immortality and by the medicines for longevity. He even became a Taoist monk after having endured an initiation to Taoism.

This initiation to Taoism is more complicated than those in Buddhism or Catholicism, as it is endured with the hands tied. For one or two weeks, the person incessantly walks around a temple repenting. The participants can rarely last until the end of seven days and nights. Those who cannot are considered as not being able to obtain Tao whereas those who complete the action end up exhausted and can have audiovisual illusions. This can appear quite strange. It is still unbelievable that all these well-known people fell into this trap of imprisonment. After several deaths, this method was removed and later replaced by the Method of Circulation, also known as the internal tablet.

In the history in China, the primary Zhou and secondary Zhou methods of circulation represent the main training practice of Taoism and the way to prolong life or being immortal. Many books were written dedicated to this method that continues to be practised today and is considered as an important secret that should never be revealed. All of these people believe that their practices were the original method. Several types of training are being rapidly developed in order to attract beginners. Some participants even develop mental illnesses from incorrect exercises. Precautions must be taken while practising this method of circulation.

It has already been proven that one cannot become immortal by exercising the method of circulation. Despite all of this, many people fall into this trap with no way out. It is urgent to explain this with scientific arguments.

Certain sensations produced during this exercise explain why it is easily linked to immortality or ascending to heaven. These sensations which were difficult to explain before, such as coldness, heat, aches, uneasiness, lightness and heaviness etc. are explained as "having initiated Qi (energy)" or even as "being able to release Qi". Other examples of this sensation is feeling a reflection of light when closing the eyes, feeling the stomach heating up, feeling a hot current through the meridian, feeling light etc. In fact, it is only a phenomenon that is brought about from not moving. After being immobile for some time, the concentration is transferred to a partial zone on the inside of the body, so that the sensation in the body is intensified. It is a simple and physical effect (see chap. I Reactions of the body while practising Standing Like a Tree).

## 6. DIFFERENCE BETWEEN STANDING LIKE A TREE AND QI GONG (QI PRACTICE)

In the book titled Theory of Chinese Qi Gong written by Ma Ji Ren and published in 1988, the author distinguishes two methods of Qi Gong: static and dynamic. Concerning the first method, he continues to say: "Standing Like a Tree is a mental method originally used in martial arts practice as a fundamental exercise. There are several of them invented by Master Wang Xiangzhai and developed in Yi Quan. In 1958, Mr. Wang Xiangzhai wrote three times to introduce this practice that is efficient for healing certain illnesses."

I must add that Master Wang Xiangzhai has never referred to Standing Like a Tree as originating from static Qi Gong. They are two completely different things. However, since everyone considers it as such, the interpretation is accepted.

Firstly, an analysis of the exercise itself can be carried out. Generally, the participants first try to enter into a static state where they concentrate on Dan Tian (around 5 cm above the navel), guiding the breathing with the mind and artificially regulating the breathing. These three elements represent the fundamental rule. After, the practice of Qi Gong requires passing through several pathways of meridian circulation (primary circulation, primary Zhou). This method stems from thought of superstition in Taoism and Buddhism and must be carefully executed as it can cause side effects if not used correctly. People who do not follow this practice are considered as having "entered into the devil's den". Mistakes are made if one tries too hard to practise the three elements and the method of circulation stated above. Without concentrating on it so intensely, no mistakes will be made. I hope that people will be able to learn from the negative experiences.

There are some common points in the method of Standing Like a Tree and Qi Gong, practised for longevity and health purposes. These two methods require staying in a fixed position. According to the analysis of existing documents, the second method is without movement and thus, purely static as it is defined as a quest for static state by controlling the brain and reducing physical energy consumption. This is done in order to get into a state of Qi Gong by using the least amount of energy possible. It does not require body movement in order to create the movement of relaxation in the muscles as with, for example, Tai Chi etc. On the other hand, the first method is static with movement at the same time. When a fixed position is kept, the movement of relaxation in the limbs is continuously produced. This movement is carried out while physically maintaining the body without moving. As such, the brain can be controlled and can also enter into a static state. If at the same time the mind is relaxed, the brain will be in a state of agitation.

After the presentation of the three main methods from Guanzi, Laozi and Emperor Huang, the summary of the method of Posture a Tree in the quest for the "Object" was created. See the table below.

| | |
|---|---|
| 3 people | Advanced : practises Tao : Intermediary : practises Tao from time to time : Beginner : does not know Tao (Laozi) |
| 3 No's | Do not walk like a horse : Do not fly like a bird : Do not move before obtaining the Object (Guanzi) ; it is dangerous to move without knowing the rules (Laozi) |
| 3 independents | Independent without moving (Laozi) : Independent by focusing the mind (Emperor Huang) : Quest for the Object through Standing Like a Tree |
| 3 observations | Without anything in order to observe the magic of things : Having in order to observe the rule : Nature is in circulation (Laozi) |
| Supreme Stage | Unify the muscles as one (Emperor Huang) : There are images and the Object (Laozi) : Connoisseurs are not afraid of the tiger |

Summary of method of Standing Like a Tree in quest for the "Object"

# 7. THE DEVELOPMENT OF STANDING LIKE A TREE IN MODERN TIMES

Standing Like a Tree was created in modern times from the basic practice of Xin Yi Quan or of (Xing Yi Quan, Yi Quan, Da Cheng Quan). It seems that Xin Yi Quan was created by Yue Fei, a well-known General during the Song Dynasty (1103-1142) and Yue Wu. However, according to Mr. Huang Xin Min in Biography of Ji Ji Ke, Ji Ji Ke, also known as Long Feng, was born in the province of Shan Xi between 1600-1680 and died when he was more 80 years old. He spent 10 years with Shao Lin Si (Temple of Shao Lin) studying martial arts and more specifically examining cock fighting. He then created martial arts that are well-kept within Shao Lin Si.

After him, these practices were divided into two categories: Henan and Shan Xi.

The third generation of Xing Yi Quan comes from one of these categories and was created by Li Luo Neng who learnt it in Shan Xi during the period 1840-1850. His students are again divided into two categories. One was formed by Chen Yi Zhai and Song Shi Rong and is called Shan Xi and the other was formed by Guo Yun Shen and Liu Qi Lan and is called He bei.

The fourth generation is called Yi Quan. It was created by Master Guo Yun Shen's student, Master Wang Xiangzhai. It is also known by the name Da Cheng Quan.

Yi Quan was the name used by master Wang Xiangzhai while he taught his apprenticeship classes in Shanghai even though he used the name Da Cheng Quan in the 40's in Beijing.

Yi Quan or Da Cheng Quan is based on the practice of Standing Like a Tree with strength test exercises, step exercises by means of rubbing, release of power, sensing sound, hand pushing and combat. Standing Like a Tree and strength testing are the basis of the practice. Da Cheng Quan concentrates on "having strength" through Standing Like a Tree, by knowing it, testing it, using it, releasing it, executing it by hand pushing and finally, mastering it by real combat.

The other use is designed for medicine, for its therapeutic health benefits and its ability to heal.

During 1950, Ze Jing Jian (1903-1989), Japanese martial arts master in Japan, started taking a class by the name of Tai Chi Quan and published in 1976 the book titled "Chinese Combat: Tai Chi Quan". In this book, he told how he had been beaten Master Wang Xiangzhai in 1940 and thus became his student.

Yu Yong Nian created the practice for good health in 1953 in Beijing. It produced spectacular healing benefits and was thus named Standing Like a Tree for healing purposes.

In 1982, the book *Method for Good Health: Standing Like a Tree* was published. It was a great success and generated many copies in Hong-Kong and elsewhere.

Guo Gui Zhi represented the Iron Shirt in the province of Shan Xi and participated in competitions for martial arts presentation at national level in 1980 and 1981. He received the golden medal for his demonstration of Da Cheng Quan. Until now, he has been the only person to represent Da Cheng Quan. On the 11th June 1981 in the newspaper, People in the Iron Shirt, an article was published titled "How to turn a sick person into a champion receiving a golden medal" where his apprenticeship was discussed in detail. He was then called president of the association for the Research of Da Cheng Quan to take Da Cheng Quan classes.

In 1884, with the permission from the commission of martial arts of Beijing, the Association of the Research of Yi Quan was created with Yao Zona Xun as the President. This organization trained a great number of high-level students and plays an important role in the development of Yi Quan.

In London, Mr. Li Jin Chuan has been using Standing Like a Tree to heal different kinds of illnesses with success since 1985. He published the book titled *The Way of Energy*, *Standing Like a Tree* in English, French, German and Spanish.

In July 1994, a group of five people from the 4th TV channel in London paid a special visit to Beijing. Master Yu Yong Nian did a presentation Standing Like a Tree. Then, they filmed ten series in Xiang Shan and in Song Shan in the Province of Henan.

In 1988 in Hong Kong, the Yi Quan association was created, whose President was Mr. Huo Zhen Huan,. This association regularly diffused statements and often invited guests from China.

The great advantage of Standing Like a Tree is the fact that it does not have any negative effects as one does not need to get into a static state, focus the mind, or regulate breathing or circulation. Taking a fixed position, controlling the number of movements and mental concentration is enough.

The following step is quite complex and consists of learning combat techniques and studying the body's mechanical activities.

Standing Like a Tree brings the effects of medicine, health and combat technique together. Its aim is the quest for the Object and to practise it, a fixed position must be maintained without a series of gestures in the form of movements. It is the image of the principles of ancient philosophy. I summarize it in the following way:

Equation of 2nd voluntary movement:

(speed = strength) x time = 1st voluntary movement
back-and-forth movement of the working muscles

(angle + mind) x time = 2nd voluntary movement
flexible movement from muscles at rest

| 730-635 B.C. | Guanzi | No movement before... | Guanzi |
|---|---|---|---|
| 571-471 B.C. | Laozi | Independent without changing | Laozi |
| 450-350 B.C. | Nei Jing | Independent in focusing on the mind | Principles of Emperor Huang |

| | | | |
|---|---|---|---|
| 369-286 B.C. | Zhuangzi | Forgetting while in a seated position | Zhuangzi chap. 6 |
| 142 | Taoist | Internal Method | Circulations : big Zhou small Zhou |
| 487-593 | Buddhist | Chan | Chan |
| 1103-1142 | Yue Fei | XinYiLiuHe Quan | Yue Fei during combat |
| 1600-1680 | Ji Ji Ke | XinYiHa | Studying cock fight |
| 1750 | Dai Bang Long | XingYi Quan | At Luo Yang |
| 1850 | Li Lao Neng | XingYi Quan | At Shan Xi |
| 1903 | Guo Yun Shen | XingYi Quan | Died in 1903 |
| 1920 | Wang Xiangzhai | Yi Quan | Shanghai : " Principles of Yi Quan " |
| 1940 | Wang Xiangzhai | DachengQuan | Beijing : " Principles of Da Cheng Quan " and " Principles of martial arts " |
| 1950 | Ze Jing Jian Yi | Tai ChiQuan | 1976 Tai ChiQuan combat techniques in China |
| 1953 | Yu Yong Nian | Standing Like a Tree | -1982 in Beijing : " Standing Like a Tree health method "; -1987 in Hong Kong : " Principles of Martial arts in Standing Like a Tree "; -1988 in Beijing : " Standing Like a Tree health method "; 1996 : " Standing Like a Tree " |
| 1985 | Lin Jin Quan | Standing Like a Tree | 1991 in England : " The Way of Energy – Standing Like a Tree " |

Chronology of Standing Like a Tree

# CHAPTER IX
# THE "OBJECT", OR THE SECOND VOLUNTARY MOVEMENT

## 1. CATEGORIES OF MOVEMENT

Standing Like a Tree is about establishing a posture and keeping it, like a tree.

The "Strength (Jin)" researched in martial arts is completely different from other types of sports. This strength is not normal strength. It is characterized by a short duration of release and I call it "intelligent strength" to distinguish it from normal strength. All types of sports need strength to be released. This strength can be understood in several ways. For example, Mr. Chen Yan Lin states: "Normal strength has a shape whilst strength in martial arts does not. The first is rectangular whereas the second is circular; the first is rough whereas the second is smooth; the first is slow and the second is fast; the first is dispersed and the second is concentrated; the first is stiff whereas the second is loose. They are different." Pure strength is Jing (according to Mr. Shi Rong Hua). Jing is the impact felt by the muscles of the body that are in proper coordination and strength is only partially released (according to Mr. Yan Tian Fang). Master Wang Xiangzhai sees it as the Object.

These slightly abstract and complex explanations are incomplete since Jing or Object have to be presented in certain forms. As such, we can try to understand them in a scientific sense. After having discussed physical changes after training, according to practice schedules, I discussed it in flexible movement in muscles at rest i.e. the secondary voluntary movement.

According to the organization of the body, anatomy distinguishes three types of muscles: smooth, cardiac and horizontal.

The muscles in the stomach, intestine, bladder, uterus and blood vessels are smooth and their flexible movement is relatively slow and long. Cardiac muscles surround the heart and their movement is relatively rapid and sharp. These two types of smooth and cardiac muscles cannot be willingly contracted. The movements they produce are thus called "involuntary movements".

The horizontal muscles are stuck to the bone and are thus called "bone muscles" e.g. the muscles in the head, face, body and limbs. Their flexible movement is rapid but they get tired quickly and can be controlled by the mind. We thus call this voluntary movement.

The bone muscles are usually separated into two groups with each one having an opposed role around the axis of the movement. One can be found on the curved surface of the joint and is called the joint's flexion muscle. The other can be found on the flat surface of the joint and is thus, called the joint's flat muscle, whose role is helping with extension. The two groups of muscles have contrasting roles but are dependent on each other.

Usually, a sport needs three conditions: speed, strength and flexible rotating movement at the same rhythm of the curved and flat muscles as well as the lever effect created by the muscles in movement rotating around the axis of the joint. This effect trains the body's movement in space and increases heartbeat. This process is called the athletic movement.

People believing in the movement of shifting, believe that a static state means speed that is equal to zero and that there is no movement when strength is not exerted. The principle of movement not existing if there is no speed or strength is applicable to objects but it is not for human activities and especially not applicable to Chinese martial arts.

A curved and flat motion (bent and stretched) is a movement. Is the body in movement when it stays in a curved or flat (bent or stretched) static state? The response is no according to normal reasoning. However, "Static State is a special case of movement". For example, Engels said: "If a heavy object is raised without moving, its potential energy is one of the forms of movement." He also said "Movement is not only shifting; it is beyond the domain of mechanical theory, a qualitative transformation." And: "All movements are done in relation to shifting in position. The higher the type of movement is, the more shifting is reduced." He continues to say: "(...) from a simple movement to thought." (Dialectics of Nature) This is also movement. What is the "movement of thinking"? After so many years of reflections and tests, I have decided that the "secondary voluntary movement" is the athletic movement of thinking i.e. the flexible movement of muscles at rest.

This theory can be described as making one part of the muscles (working muscles) contract while the bigger part of the muscles (muscles at rest) is in a state of rest. For example, when a joint is in flexion, the muscle being flexed is the one that works and the flat muscle is the one that is at rest and vice versa when the joint is flat, the first one becomes the muscle at rest and the second becomes the muscle at work. The muscles that are being flexed and stretched contract alternately, not at the same time. It is a law of movement of shifting for animals. Obviously, there is an exception for humans who go through a special training.

According to the principle stated above, I will now summarize the following points:

-STANDARDS OF MOVEMENT

There are two standards: the subjective standard and the objective and scientific standard.

We usually believe that movement is created by shifting in position by stretching or bending the body and a static state is a relatively fixed position. This is a subjective standard in terms of the principle of movement corresponding to a position. Furthermore, movement increases heartbeat, a common point in the body for all movements.

We can now qualify the objective and physical standard as a quantity of movement in relation to the increase in the number of beats without counting the movement relative to position since Standing Like a Tree in a fixed position also increases the number of beats.

## SYSTEM OF MOVEMENT

According to each gesture of the body, the two systems of body movement can be distinguished:
- System acquired at birth that everyone has: the primary voluntary movement, flexible movement in the muscles at work
- System to be taught after birth: the secondary voluntary movement, flexible movement in the muscles at rest.

### -PROCESS OF MOVEMENT

Three types of flexible movement:

### -Alternative contraction

Movement from habitual shifting e.g. walking, jogging, gymnastics etc. that consist in respectively and alternately contracting the muscles of flexion and extension.

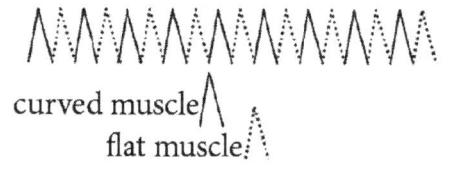

$$\wedge\wedge\wedge\wedge\wedge\wedge\wedge\wedge\wedge\wedge\wedge\wedge$$
curved muscle /\
flat muscle /\

### -SOLE CONTRACTION

This has two types: permanent and rapid
Permanent contraction alone:
The body is kept in a fixed position by the muscles of flexion and extension in sole and permanent contraction. For example, the four

limbs of the body in a fixed position of Standing Like a Tree, the working muscles are in the movement of sole and permanent contraction. (drawing below)

Muscles at work

-SOLE RAPID CONTRACTION

This is a special phenomenon in the practice of Standing Like a Tree: the two legs are bent at a defined angle, after some time (usually after 20 to 30 minutes), one can touch certain leg muscles in the sole rapid contraction movement. This movement is done in an automatic, high frequency and wave-like manner. Master Wang Xiangzhai characterizes it as "the muscles are like a startled snake" (see drawing below)

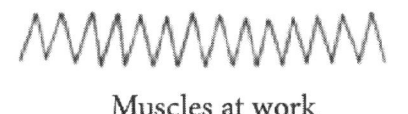

Muscles at work

These two types of movement of contraction are created in an automatic way without the brain's intervention. Since there is no change in the system of movement, they form part of a voluntary movement by the muscles at work i.e. primary voluntary movement.

- SIMULTANEOUS CONTRACTION

During the movement of contraction carried out by the muscles at work, the mental activities of contraction are added (chap. IV) done by the muscles at rest. This contraction has to be done by the brain which controls the muscles at rest. It consequently changes the system of movement and thus, is categorized as secondary voluntary movement which is composed of three categories:

-PERMANENT CONTRACTION OF THE MUSCLES AT WORK + RAPID CONTRACTION OF THE MUSCLES AT REST (SEE DRAWING BELOW).

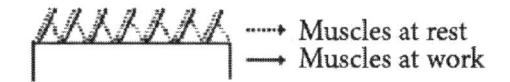

⋯→ Muscles at rest
→ Muscles at work

-PERMANENT CONTRACTION OF MUSCLES AT WORK + SLOW CONTRACTION OF MUSCLES AT REST (SEE DRAWING BELOW)

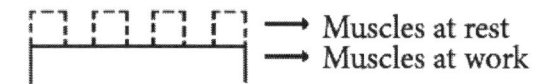

→ Muscles at rest
→ Muscles at work

-PERMANENT CONTRACTION OF MUSCLES AT WORK + PERMANENT CONTRACTION OF MUSCLES AT REST (SEE DRAWING BELOW)

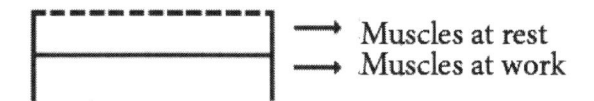

→ Muscles at rest
→ Muscles at work

The three types of contraction listed above can be verified by touching with the hands, by visual observation and by the change in beats.

## -MECHANISM OF THE CREATION OF MOVEMENT

Since the mechanisms of the nervous system in the brain to create these three types of flexible movement are different, the corresponding physical change as well as their actual role are not the same.

For example, voluntary movement in the muscles at work exists from birth and everyone is able to do it without needing the brain's intervention, whilst voluntary movement of the muscles at rest must be learnt.

At the beginning of the apprenticeship, beginners should concentrate as much as possible and let their brain guide them in order to control the flexible movement. This is of course difficult to master at first: we forget about the left side if we are concentrating on the right and vice versa.

However, if a specific rhythm starting with one part gradually increasing to the entire body is followed, after some time, it can be mastered. As such, I have separated voluntary muscle movement into two categories; Primary Voluntary Movement and Secondary Voluntary Movement.

## 2. PRIMARY VOLUNTARY MOVEMENT

Primary Voluntary Movement is adapted to all kinds of flexible movement whether they be active or passive, voluntary or only carried out by the working muscles, which facilitate changes in the angles of the body's joints or shifts in position and produce changes in breathing, circulation and metabolism. When movement has reached a certain level, most people maintain the same pulse. This type of movement is specific to animals and man.

For example: in walking, jogging, gymnastics, weight-lifting, all types of ball games, martial arts etc.

The system in charge of the movements carried out by working muscles of the body stated above remain unchanged despite changes in speed and strength. This movement alone is primary voluntary

movement characterized by the following formula:
> (speed + strength) x time = movement of shifting

## 3. SECONDARY VOLUNTARY MOVEMENT

This type of movement that is only activated from the mind without changing the angles of the body's joints changes the movement system and belongs to the domain of the flexible movement done by resting muscles. This is called secondary voluntary movement i.e. static position movement which is characterized by the following formula:
> (angle + mind) x time = static position movement

The respective joint angles and limbs remain fixed. In this way, the working muscles carry out certain types of flexible movement and the muscles at rest also carry out contraction movements through language, words or mental activities (role of the 2nd nervous system).

This movement causes the pulse to increase and activates metabolism in the body by using the two types of muscles (working and resting muscles). The effect is thus, called secondary voluntary movement.

Flexible movement in the resting muscles is the result of active, free and high-intensity agitation effects that are transmitted by the brain's nervous system. This system is created through training the resting muscles in order to take advantage of the hidden ability in the body and improve human health. It can only be mastered by training after birth which is what makes it different from the primary voluntary movement.

During practice, a fixed position is maintained without adding mental activity for contraction. Pulse is increased as the muscle's resistance against the body's weight causes certain movements of contraction. This is the characteristic of primary voluntary movement. Mental activities are added while maintaining the same posture from the start.

This makes the resting muscles contract which also increases heartbeat and is characteristic of the secondary voluntary movement. We can conclude by saying that without changing the angles of posture we change the movement system via mental intervention. Therefore, Standing Like a Tree is composed of two activities: one is physical and the other is mental.

## 4. CHANGE IN HEARTBEAT IN SECONDARY VOLUNTARY MOVEMENT

### A. CHANGE IN HEARTBEAT IN SECONDARY VOLUNTARY MOVEMENT IN A SEATED POSITION

In order to observe the phenomenon of change in heartbeat in the secondary voluntary movement, a 45-year old masculine participant was chosen. His posture is as follows: calmly seated on a chair keeping a fixed position with his feet placed on the floor forming a 90° angle between the thigh and the leg. The knee joint is not leaning to the left or right, the two arms fall freely with the body in a vertical position without trying to form any particular posture.

In this way, after 10 minutes, he starts to practise the flexible movement with his left leg i.e. secondary voluntary movement. The result of the heartbeats after 4 minutes of training is presented in the graph below:

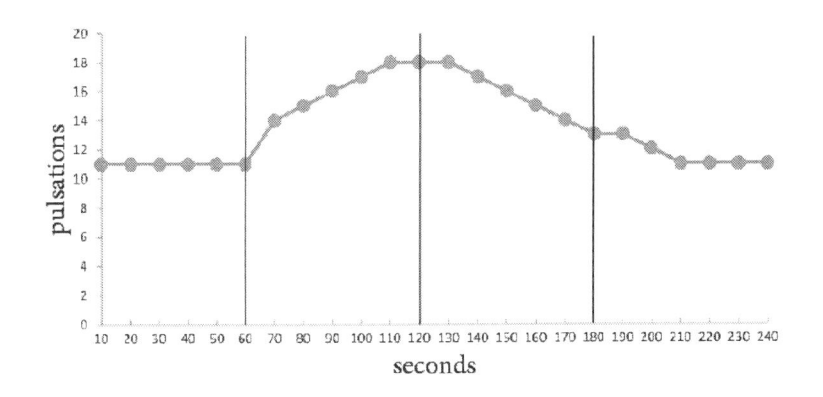

| Item | Before exercise | Leg in movement | First minute after exercise | Second minute after exercise |
|---|---|---|---|---|
| Time in seconds | 10, 20, 30, 40, 50, 60 | 70, 80, 90 100, 110, 120 | 130, 140, 150, 160, 170, 180 | 190, 200, 210, 220, 230, 240 |
| Pulse measured | 11, 11, 11, 11, 11, 11 | 14, 15, 16, 17, 18, 18 | 18, 17, 16, 15, 14, 13 | 13, 12, 11, 11, 11, 11 |
| Total heartbeats in 1 minute | 66 | 98 | 93 | 69 |
| Difference compared to before the exercise |  | +32 | +27 | +3 |

Change in heartbeat in secondary voluntary movement in a seated position

The previous table shows that during the first minute while in a seated position the heartbeats are at 11 beats per 10 seconds and 66 per minute. From 70 seconds, secondary voluntary movement takes place by contraction movement being initiated by the mind for the resting muscles in both the legs. Pulse immediately increases; after 120 seconds it reaches to 18 beats per 10 seconds and 98 per minute; corresponding to an increase of 32 seconds compared to the heartbeats before the exercise. After 130 seconds, the exercise is over and the pulse decreases to 210 seconds and then goes back to its initial state.

### B. CHANGE IN HEARTBEAT IN SECONDARY VOLUNTARY MOVEMENT IN A STANDING POSITION

To observe the change in pulse in Standing Like a Tree between contracting movements and non-contracting movements (primary vs. secondary voluntary movement) the small step posture was used (see image below) and the changes between before and after the exercise were noted.

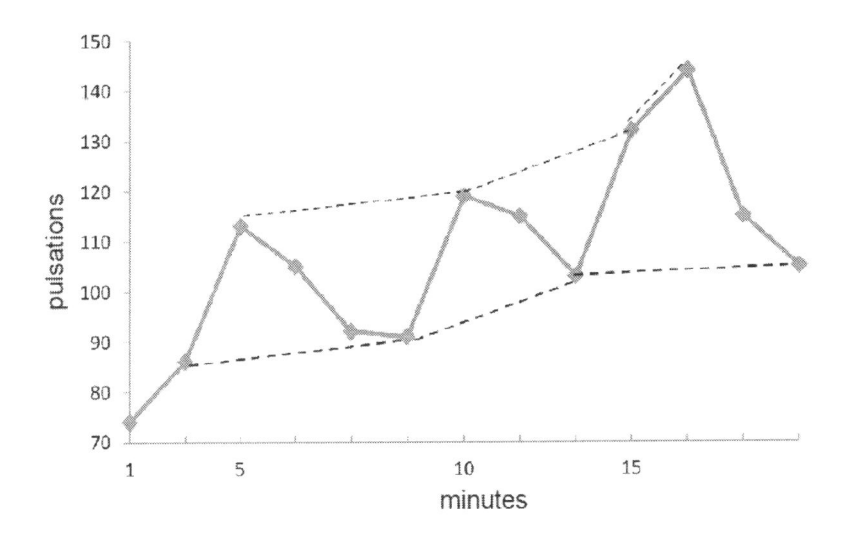

The graph above shows pulse at 74/minute before the exercise and 86/minute after 4 minutes of exercise corresponding to an increase of 12 beats. From the fifth minute, contraction is practised for 1 minute and pulse immediately reaches 113/minute corresponding to an increase of 27 beats in one minute of training and an increase of 39 beats compared to the heartbeat measured before the exercise. After 6 minutes of training, the exercise is over and the heartbeat decreases to 105/minute, then 91/minute at 7 minutes and 91/minute at 9 minutes. This highlights the difference between the two types of voluntary movements.

After 10 minutes, a second session of secondary voluntary training is initiated again, this time lasting 1 minute. Heartbeat immediately measures 119/minute, an increase of 28 beats compared to the 9th minute and 45 beats compared to the beginning of the exercise. It reaches 115/minute at 11 minutes and 103/minute at 14 minutes.

After 15 minutes, secondary voluntary movement training is restarted for a duration of 2 minutes. Heartbeat rises immediately to 132/minute, then increases by 12 beats from the first minute and by 70 beats compared to the beginning of the exercise.

On the previous graph a significant change in heartbeat is noticed between the two types of voluntary movement. Increase is proportional to the amount time of exercise, Standing Like a Tree is practised if the activity of contraction is not added. This is shown in the previous graph where the dotted line at the top represents permanent, sole contraction movement of the working muscles.

In the same position, without changing the body's movement or the relative angles, the resting muscles are activated by the mind, heartbeat rapidly increases and then decreases after stopping (previous graph, dotted line at the bottom).

This proves that in a defined posture, there is only one part of the muscles in a contracting movement whereas the other part is at rest. The aim of the secondary voluntary movement is to develop the resting muscles in order to increase the quality of training.

The graph also shows that after one minute of exercising the secondary voluntary movement, the increase in heartbeat is at 27 to 29 and 36 to 58 compared to the exercise before. This proves that the longer the duration of the exercise, the more significant the increase in heartbeat is. However, it is not advised to exercise for too long.

In the graph on the following page, changes in heartbeat are observed every 10 seconds from the 14th minute.

According to the graph, after 14 minutes of exercise, the body remains in the primary voluntary movement for the working muscles. Heartbeat is generally measured at 17 except from the fourth round of 10 seconds where it measured as 18 beats. Therefore, altogether, the rate of heartbeat is at 103 / minute. From the 15th minute, 2 minutes after the secondary voluntary movement is started, there is a rapid increase in pulse from 17 to 20, 21 to 23 and then 24 on the fifth round of 10 seconds i.e. the 110th second. At this time, movement intensity is at its highest. Then, for the rest of the exercise, pulse remains at 24 until the 180th second after stopping and then later returns to 20 and then to 19 after the 230th second.

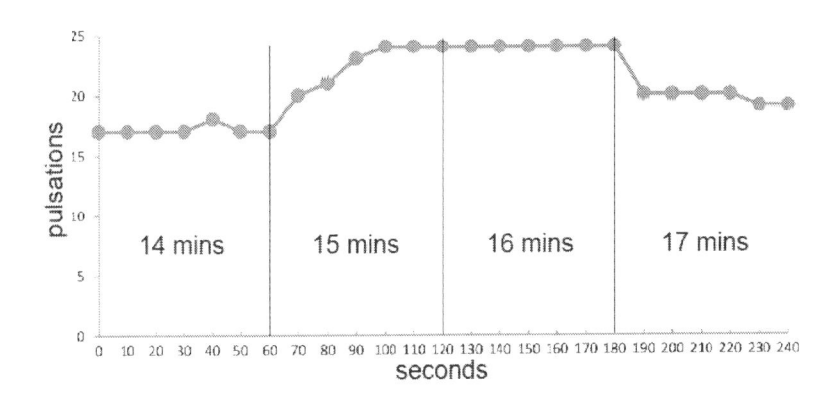

## 5. SERIES OF TRAINING IN STANDING LIKE A TREE

Using these three essential conditions: angle, mind and duration, as references, the series of training in the following diagram was created.

According to the diagram, the three axes, angle, mind and duration, form the best way for training without speed or external strength.

The axes for angle and mind show that Standing Like a Tree is an exercise that uses a posture with a fixed angle and mind activity. During the exercise, all the joints of the body are in positions with pre-determined angles.

This forms the external aspect of the practice as this position imposes the external condition to train the working muscles that can be summarized by the word "Training". At the same time, the mind needs to be activated. This activity is summarized by the word "Mind" or "Thinking" and is defined as the active training of the resting muscles. The activities of Shape and Mind must be combined as one.

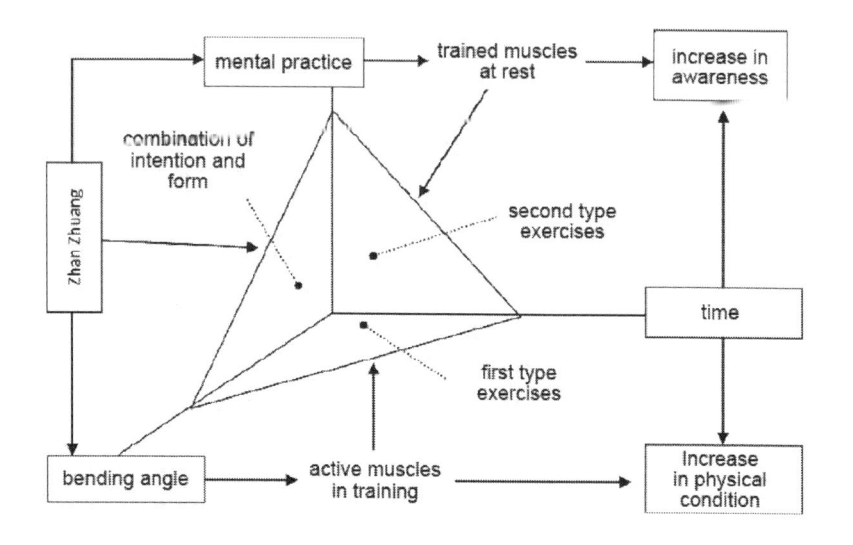

```
              mental practice ──► trained muscles ──► increase in
          ▲                          at rest              awareness
          │                                                  ▲
     combination of                                          │
     intention and                    second type            │
         form                         exercises             │
   ┌──────────┐                                              │
   │          │                                              │
   │ Zhan     │                                              │
   │ Zhuang   │                                          ┌──────┐
   │          │                                          │ time │
   │          │                                          └──────┘
   └──────────┘                                              │
                                       first type           │
                                       exercises             │
          │                                                  │
          ▼                                                  ▼
   ┌──────────────┐    active muscles         ┌─────────────────┐
   │ bending angle│──►  in training    ──────►│   Increase      │
   └──────────────┘                           │  in physical    │
                                              │   condition     │
                                              └─────────────────┘
```

How is this done? A balance needs to be found between the following elements:

1. Absence of the mind and neglecting shape.
2. Absence of the mind and putting emphasis on shape.
3. Neglecting the mind and shape at the same time.
4. Neglecting the mind and putting emphasis on shape.
5. Putting emphasis on the mind and neglecting shape.
6. Putting emphasis on the mind and shape at the same time.

Amongst these elements, 1 and 2 belong to the primary voluntary movement and 3, 4, 5 and 6 to the secondary voluntary movement.

## A. DEMANDS OF THE PRIMARY VOLUNTARY MOVEMENT IN STANDING LIKE A TREE

For this, as indicated in the previous diagram, a well-defined position needs to be maintained according to the axes of angle and time which determine the primary voluntary movement. Standing Like a Tree is the way to train the working muscles. The rest of the muscles are in a state of relaxation but are not limp; they are tight but not rigid, and light with a good state of mind.

It can also be said that the limbs do not move in order to reduce the effect of mental agitation due to the careful vigilance of the body to ensure that the brain is able to control the exercise and the body's safety. Actually, the action of contraction and the brain at rest working are done at the same time. This method plays an important role in health. Increases in angle and duration can help reinforce health.

## B. DEMANDS OF THE SECONDARY VOLUNTARY MOVEMENT IN STANDING LIKE A TREE

Here, as indicated in the diagram before, a well-defined position needs to be maintained while adding mental activity according to the axes of angle and time which characterize the secondary voluntary movement. This method of Standing Like a Tree is used for training the resting and working muscles and is used to develop the nervous system by making the resting muscles work, in order to create a new system of movement.

The mental activities of the secondary voluntary movement are:

- 1. Training the resting muscles via contraction
- 2. Training the nerves via a bonding activity.
- 3. Training the muscles by flexion and extension.
- 4. Training the mind by activities of pulling and gripping.

Prolonging mental activity and duration develop physical state and intelligence simultaneously.

Intelligence is attributed to the mechanical knowledge of the body's activity. For example, it studies the problems of muscle contraction together with the following points:

- How to use strength in order to increase the length of applied strength;

- How to use different strengths;
- How to distribute strength, for example, in which places should it be used and in which should it not be used;
- What direction and length of strength: strength on both the sides or on one side, its central position, change in its speed, interruption on continuity, strength and opposed strength, horizontal or perpendicular.

All the knowledge put together gives the aspect of what is called "Jing" (Strength), that the great master Wang Xiangzhai called "Object". It belongs to the domain of intelligence and I call it the secondary involuntary movement.

| 1 | Training in a crouched position | Suitable for people having a low level of fitness |
| --- | --- | --- |
| 2 | Training in a seated position | Auxiliary method for method 3 for people with case 1 |
| 3 | Training while standing | Basis of Standing Like a Tree |
| 4 | Training while walking | No rubbing as a basis of movement training |
| 5 | Strength-testing | 1. Partial<br>2. Complete<br>3. Release |
| 6 | Sensing sound | 1. Combined with strength-testing<br>2. Sound released is different to normal sound |
| 7 | Pushing of arms | 1. Only one hand;<br>2. Two hands<br>3. Fixed<br>4. In movement |
| 8 | Combat | 1. With bare hands<br>2. With equipment |

Da Cheng summary of Standing Like a Tree

## 6. APPLICATION OF STANDING LIKE A TREE

### A. SPORTS DOMAIN

Standing Like a Tree as sports helps with the development of research for several studies on man and provides a different aspect of other types of sport by analyzing physical change in the body.

### B. MEDICAL AND HEALTH DOMAIN

The effect of Standing Like a Tree in Medicine and improvement in health is well-certified in practice. Numerous illnesses that were impossible to be treated were cured by this method. A long duration of this practice reinforces health, slows ageing and increases productivity.

### C. TRAINING DOMAIN

By applying Standing Like a Tree to conventional sports training, one completes practices in movement. For people who include the principle of secondary voluntary movement, results can be significantly increased.

### D. REACTION FROM ACTIONS REQUIRING LITTLE EFFORT

Standing Like a Tree increases reaction ability for actions requiring little effort. This has a high value in the aeronautics sector. According to a study, someone who carries out an action that requires great effort reacts to weak light in 1 to 3 seconds on average whereas with action requiring little effort this reaction takes more than 20 seconds. After training, this ability of reaction is only at 4 seconds.

### E. STRENGTH RECOVERY

By applying the principle of relaxation of the mind, this method helps recover strength and stop fatigue.

### F. INCREASE IN PRODUCTIVITY

Not only does this method heal certain illnesses and reinforce one's state of health but it also promotes good academic results, develops intelligence as well as increases productivity in studying and working.

## 7. CONCLUSION

### A. IMMOBILITY IS ALSO A MOVEMENT

Generally, we think that shifting is needed for movement. The contrary is highlighted by showing that immobility is a state of special exercise. The movements are divided into two categories: movement by shifting and static movement. Their formulae are as follows:

(speed + strength) x time = movement by shifting;

Speed and strength change but the principle of the exercise remains the same.

(angle + mind) x time = static movement of position;

The mind and the exercise system changes but the angle does not.

### B. NEW CATEGORY OF VOLUNTARY MOVEMENT

After a normative study of conditions, the system, process and the mechanisms of human movement, I created a category of voluntary movement by explaining the movement of flexion and extension by the working muscles and the movement of contraction by the resting muscles. This corresponds to the primary and secondary voluntary movement.

## C. MENTAL ACTIVITIES

In light of the changes in rhythm and pulse, I pointed out that in a static position an opposed strength is created due to one's own weight that creates flexible movement in the working muscles. This ability is possessed from birth. It increases heartbeat and is called "primary voluntary movement". Certain mental activities are added to this movement in order to change the system of movement by executing contracting movement in the resting muscles. As such, pulse is also increased and this movement is thus called "secondary voluntary movement".

## D. EXERCISE OF THOUGHT

The change in pulse shows the existence of the system of exercise of thought. It creates a new system of movement: secondary voluntary movement. This name is perfectly suitable for the different exercises practised in the domain of martial arts in China.

## E. SMALL MOVEMENT – HIGH-LEVEL SPORT

Engels said in The Dialectics of Nature: "A movement is not just shifting; it is also a certain qualitative change that is beyond the mechanical domain." "All movements are in relation to certain shifts. The smaller the shift is, the higher the level is." Standing Like a Tree does not require shifting the body but a qualitative change on the inside of the body.

The activities of contraction, liaison, pulling, rubbing etc. must be well-executed as they form the process of this change. During practice, change in height in the body is measured in cm whilst shifting of the centre of gravity is measure in mm. Measuring change in the mind is impossible, even in microns. This shows that the higher the level or type of movement is, the less shifting takes place.

### F. MOVING IN IMMOBILITY

Master Wang Xiangzhai said: "It is better to move less than more; it is better to not move than to move less; moving while being immobile is the movement of creation." This understanding provides the basis of the theory of Standing Like a Tree.

### G. REGULATION OF PULSE AND BREATHING

I show that "It is better to move slowly that quickly; immobility is better than a slow movement. Moving while being immobile is a normal movement that increases heartbeat and breathing without creating feelings of suffocation or lack of oxygen". This approach has resolved the contradiction between the increasing pulse and the simultaneous difficulty in breathing in the practice of the movement of ordinary shifting.

Made in the USA
San Bernardino, CA
20 February 2016